PROPEL

AN ANTHOLOGY OF NEW POETRY

Selected Poems from Propel Magazine 2022–24

PROPEL MAGAZINE
EDITOR-IN-CHIEF — ANTHONY ANAXAGOROU
MANAGING EDITOR — PATRICIA FERGUSON
PRODUCER — TOM MACANDREW

PROPEL MAGAZINE IS MADE POSSIBLE BY THE SUPPORT OF OUR PARTNERS:

THE FENTON ARTS TRUST
BRADFORD LITERATURE FESTIVAL
LEDBURY POETRY CRITICS
OLD POSSUM'S PRACTICAL TRUST

Published by Propel Magazine Limited
PO Box 78744
London, N11 9FG

All rights reserved.

Introduction ©Anthony Anaxagorou, 2024. Copyright in each individual work in this anthology lies with the authors of those works. Each of the literary works in this publication is reproduced with the permission of its author. The anthology as a collective work ©Propel Magazine Limited, 2024.

The rights of each of the contributors to be identified as authors of their respective works in this anthology have been asserted by them in accordance with section 77 of the Copyright, Designs and Patents Act 1988.

A CIP record for this title is available from the British Library.

This book is in copyright. Subject to statutory exception and to provisions of relevant collective licensing agreements, no reproduction of any part may take place without the written permission of Propel Magazine Limited.

First edition published 2024
ISBN: 9781068671227

Typeset in Futura and Adobe Garamond
Printed and bound by Short Run Press

CONTENTS

FOREWORD BY PROPEL EDITOR-IN-CHIEF ANTHONY ANAXAGOROU	*i*
WISH BEAR, *Jo Bratten*	*1*
SALOBREÑA, *Tom Bailey*	*3*
THE CHILDREN HAVE FORGOTTEN TO BE AFRAID, *Sarah Terkaoui*	*4*
EXACTLY AS MUCH, *Olive Franklin*	*5*
BURST ME INTO SONG, *Isabelle Baafi*	*6*
PRAYING TO ÂU CO AFTER MY FIRST CERVICAL SCREENING, *Natalie Linh Bolderston*	*8*
[SOMETIMES I THINK I'M THE WRONG TYPE OF GAY], *Serge ♆ Neptune*	*9*
GOOD IMMIGRANT, *Yanita Georgieva*	*10*
ACCORDING TO MARTIN, *Simon Maddrell*	*11*
THERE IS NO BELIEF WITHOUT UNBELIEF, *Sanah Ahsan*	*12*
FROM WORK POEMS: 10, *Charlotte Geater*	*15*
INEVITABILITIES, *Oluwaseun Olayiwola*	*16*
MEN'S TOILET HAIKU, *Jackson Phoenix Nash*	*18*
DEAD FOX, *Dide*	*19*
TEACH JACKDAWS AVIONICS, *Taz Rahman*	*20*
AT BARROW HILL, *Natalie Burdett*	*21*
OVER THE BONES OF THE DEAD, *Alex Jenkins*	*22*
RADISH MONODY, *Ben Philipps*	*24*
RELATIONSHIP AS COVERED RESERVOIR, *Paul Stephenson*	*25*
I, *Irum Fazal*	*26*

NATAL NOISES, FATAL FLAWS, *Muskaan Razdan*	*29*
EN PLEIN AIR, *Clíodhna Bhreatnach*	*30*
AL-ASRAR, *Ali Fitzpatrick*	*31*
POEM BEGINNING WITH A LINE BY AR AMMONS, *Caspar Bryant*	*32*
THE FROG WIFE, *Livia Franchini*	*33*
HOW TO LEAVE, *Ciara Maguire*	*34*
IN THE DISTANCES OF THIS COUNTRY, *Rojbîn Arjen Yiğit*	*35*
WAREHOUSE, *Tom McLaughlin*	*36*
انار, *Mohammad S. Razai*	*37*
LOVE WHITE HOT LIKE GOD WHITE HOT LIKE GRIEF WHITE, *Shayna Kowalczyk*	*38*
AUGURY, *Miruna Fulgeanu*	*41*
WHAT I HEAR WHEN SISTERS COMPARE UPBRINGINGS, *Kayla Marie Troy*	*42*
SEMI-ERMINE, *Richard O'Brien*	*43*
CODEX DREAM, *Lucie Richter-Mahr*	*44*
THE REMAINS OF SKY, *Memoona Zahid*	*45*
FOREIGN BODIES, *Iulia David*	*46*
ABSEAS, *Martha Aroha Челок*	*48*
LITTLE IRONIES, *Jared Collins*	*49*
CAPACITY, *Rebecca McCutcheon*	*50*
LIKE A CHILD IN A STORY BOOK, *Rachel Curzon*	*51*
IMPALA, *Caitlin Tina Jones*	*55*
DREAMCATCHER, *Zahra Rafiq*	*56*
WHAT SHOULD WE DO WITH OUR SUPERSTITIOUS FATHERS, *Lucille Mona Ling*	*57*

CHOOSING JEWELS, *Francesca Brooks*	60
TOPSOIL, *Shakeema Edwards*	62
BITCH RIVER, *Ellora Sutton*	63
TURLOUGH, *David Nash*	64
SIREN, *Karan Chambers*	66
SONNET (WITH AN UNTRANSLATED COPY OF *FRAGOLETTA*), *VJ René*	67
MORNING, *Aleja Taddesse*	68
BEAT, *Marina Scott*	71
HOMESICKNESS, *Elontra Hall*	72
WHO WE MOURN, *Carson Wolfe*	73
LANDSCAPE WITH VAPOUR-SPRAYED AUBERGINES, *Adam Heardman*	74
NEGATIVE CAPABILITY & THE TOMATOES, *Claire Collison*	76
FINAL DESTINATION, *Courtney Conrad*	77
THE BODY IS NOT AN APOLOGY, *Titilayo Farukuoye*	78
CHIPPED SOUND, *Mark Saunders*	79
PERMANENT, *Cat Turhan*	80
PROTEUS IN MOURNING, *Dominic Leonard*	82
METEMPSYCHOSIS, *Alana Chase*	87
POSTPARTUM, *Erica Hesketh*	88
AUBURN, *Millie Guille*	89
NOT ABOUT URBAN EXPLORERS, *Stuart Charlesworth*	90
DREAMBABY, *Chloe Elliott*	94
PRIN / CESS / PARK / MAN / OR, *Gemma Barnett*	95
SIMULATION, *Eira Elisabeth Murphy*	99
FATHERS WHO WERE SOLDIERS CAN'T PLAY HIDE AND SEEK, IT'S IN THE MANIFESTO SIS, *Yaz Nin*	101

IN THE ROCKPOOL, *Kristian Evans*	*102*
SEVEN OTHER THINGS GEORGE FLOYD IS DOING RIGHT NOW, *Thembe Mvula*	*103*
THE IRISH QUESTION, *Fin Keegan*	*107*
HELL IS A DUMP INTO THE PYMMES BROOK, *Francis-Xavier Mukiibi*	*108*
STRATHCLYDE PENSION FUND, *Silas Curtis*	*110*
DAUGHTER, IN RELATION TO, *Betty Doyle*	*113*
NOTE ON PASSING, *Leyla Çolpan*	*114*
AMIANTHUS INCEPTION OF DYSFUNCTION, *Cogwheel*	*115*
BIG UTOPIA, *Caroline Wiygul*	*116*
WITH, *Alia Zapparova*	*118*
SOUNDING SOIL, *Agata Maslowska*	*119*
ST. FRANCIS, *Shani Cadwallender*	*121*
THE FIRST 7 DAYS AS A WITCH, *Natalie Moores*	*125*
A WORMHOLE IS, *Debmalya Bandyopadhyay*	*126*
A QUESTIONNAIRE FOR THE FURIES, *Katherine Collins*	*127*
SELF-PORTRAIT AS MY GHOST, WHO WILL EVENTUALLY HAUNT YOU, *Rachel Bruce*	*128*
ST NICHOLAS REFUSES HIS MOTHER'S MILK ON FASTING DAYS, *Aysar Ghassan*	*130*
CORRIGENDUM, *JP Seabright*	*131*
THE BEATIFICATION OF CATHERINE OF SIENA, *Sam Furlong*	*132*
YOU COME THROUGH THE SOIL, *Jon Alex Miller*	*133*
THE MEN IN COMPANY VANS WHO GIVE LIFTS TO AWAY MATCHES, *Patrick O'Donoghue*	*134*
QUEER CLIMATE, *Julia Ireland*	*135*

ODE TO PIERRE, *Iain Bleakley*	*139*
EASTER LEAVE, *Megan McKie-Smith*	*140*
WHITE BREAD WHITE SWANS, *Lou Hill*	*142*
THE STATUE, *Henry St Leger*	*144*
UNDER, *Rafael Mendes*	*145*
MAYBE THE SUN, *Ian Irwin*	*146*
SELF-PORTRAIT AS A FAILED EXORCISM, *Deborah Finding*	*148*
WHEN I WOKE UP THIS MORNING I TRIPPED OVER DAD, *Anna Shelton*	*150*
BECAUSE IT'S MUD SEASON AT THE GIRLS' FACILITY, *Eve Ellis*	*151*
TO THE BLACKENED FIELD, *Tracey McEvoy*	*153*
CROWN THE MOMENT, *Adam Clifford*	*157*
BELLY BUTTON ODE, *Olivia Tuck*	*158*
IT'S GOOD WE KNEW, *Oenone Thomas*	*159*
BARBIE GOES TO THE GYNAE, *Amy Dugmore*	*160*
FROM *DÉRIVE*, *Alex Priestley*	*161*
THE DEVIL HAS A PLAN / FOR US, *Ewan John*	*162*
THE LAST SUPPER, *Nige Tassell*	*163*
MIRROR, *Eugene O'Hare*	*164*
BIG TED, *Karen Green*	*165*
DEATH OF A SWIMMING TEACHER, *Christopher Tracy*	*166*
MOTHS, *Maya Caspari*	*169*
LICENCE APPLICATION, *Mave Fellowes*	*172*
CHE GUEVARA PLANTS A TREE IN CEYLON, *S. Niroshini*	*173*
LEAVING THE CITY, *Zain Rishi*	*175*

SELF PORTRAIT AS AGATHA CHRISTIE NOVEL, *AV Bridgwood*   *176*

ANACHRONISTIC, *Emmett Coleman*   *177*

GEEZERDOM, *Em Gray*   *178*

SEAHORSE GRAMMAR: CYDIPPE, *Michelle Szobody*   *179*

DIARY OF A FRONTIER BRIDE, *Rebecca Ferrier*   *180*

WATER TORTURE, *Marcia Hindson*   *182*

CONTRIBUTORS   *185*

FOREWORD

In late 2021 I was having a Zoom with one of my mentees, when after reading the latest draft of one of her poems I said, 'this could easily be in a magazine, it's brilliant.' She solemnly replied, 'It's been turned down by all the big ones… I don't think I'm a strong enough name yet.' I thought, does this mean poetry is more a popularity contest than an endeavour to write interesting poems? Or is the talent pool literally so small that only a handful of people know what they're doing? Who was/is the arbiter of quality and artfulness? The answer, to my mind at least, is that poetry is a highly subjective artform that resists the machinations of capitalism while still producing more than it consumes, meaning the infrastructure employed to disseminate and preserve it becomes fraught. This leads to editors having to make difficult decisions so as not to unsettle their subscriber-base. Some magazines do showcase a healthy mix of emerging poets, alongside some of the more established names, yet it's most likely the bigger names who not only sell the magazine but fortify its reputation.

At some point in that meeting I said, '…there should be a place which just prioritises new poets.' After I considered the pros and cons – will people read a magazine which features poets they haven't encountered before? Why has nobody done this in the past, and if they have why don't I know about it? How will quality be decided upon, and how would we ensure the selection process is democratic while still monetarily valuing the time of the editor(s) and the work of the poets? I then took to X to see what people thought of the initiative that would soon become *Propel Magazine*.

The Poetry Review, *Poetry London*, *Magma*, *The Rialto*, *Butcher's Dog*, *fourteen poems*, *PN Review*, *Granta*, *Gutter*, *The Stinging Fly*, *Banshee* and formerly *bath magg* all do a great job at keeping poetry's ecosystem busy and up-to-date. But the poetry world is irregular, insular, nepotistic, and aesthetically/poetically quite conservative. So how then does a poet with no presence on the national stage announce themselves to readers and fellow writers? Where it's common for editors to solicit poems from poets who already have a profile, having a free magazine exclusively for those who are less frequently considered due to their publishing record seemed like an important feature.

If you speak to anyone working in British poetry today, you'll eventually end up lamenting the precarity of publishing, teaching, and performing, while also noting the ever-limited space poetry now has for criticism and review. Over the past five years, many of the country's traditional channels have done away with sections they would typically assign to poetry. *The Guardian* still publish their minuscule quarterly round-up, but *The Sunday Times*, *The Telegraph* and *The New Statesman*, which readers conventionally would turn to for keeping up to date with new work, have all moved away from covering poetry.

The anxiety I often grapple with is whether there'll be a robust enough cultural place in the future for poetry to exist on its own terms, and for readers to discover work that appeals to them without relying on prize lists or puff reviews. The recent change in appetite from commercial publishers will most likely see a shift in what's commissioned, along with the monetary value assigned to buying poetry manuscripts. Commercial presses tend to chase the zeitgeist, focus on what's sellable, and dare I say it 'accessible', and on what they assume readers across the board want from poetry. But will the vagaries of market populism, along with the lyric's stronghold become the overarching cocktail to steer poetry into the next decade?

The long-term aim of *Propel* is to help establish a first-base for tomorrow's poets. For readers and fellow poets alike to have an open and accessible resource that allows them to browse, listen, read and explore previous issues. I'd like to extend my massive thanks not only to the poets who feature in these pages, but also to all the editors who've laboured over submissions and introduced their issues with grace and generosity. The homogenisation of poetry has negative effects, so the regular change in editorship with each issue acts to reset our stage, allowing for a more diverse and expansive curatorial archive by the end of the magazine's life.

As ever I'm eternally indebted to the wonderful *Propel* team – Patricia Ferguson without whom there would be nothing to write about or celebrate, and Tom MacAndrew who handles a spreadsheet and my onslaught of 'new ideas' the way Federer handled Centre Court! We're hugely grateful to our funders and supporters. Securing private sponsorship to enable the *Propel* team to get paid for their time, alongside the poets and editors is integral to the ethos of the magazine. Yet as many readers will know, the current economic climate is pretty grim with the arts and culture sector taking a big hit in its budgets and funding channels. With this in mind we're introducing a subscription model with monthly bonus content and discounts for our members, aiming to establish a sustainable poetry community for emerging poets and discerning readers, while keeping the core magazine free and open to access.

I hope that within this first omnibus edition you discover poems which stir, move, arouse, provoke, confound and revitalise you. I'm sure that in the very near future, we'll be reading much more from many of the brilliant poets featured in these pages.

— Anthony Anaxagorou
Editor-in-Chief, *Propel Magazine*
August 2024

ISSUE ONE

September 2022
Edited by Mary Jean Chan

MARY JEAN CHAN is the author of *Flèche*, published by Faber & Faber (2019) and Faber USA (2020). *Flèche* won the 2019 Costa Book Award for Poetry and was shortlisted in 2020 for the International Dylan Thomas Prize, the John Pollard Foundation International Poetry Prize, the Jhalak Prize and the Seamus Heaney Centre First Collection Poetry Prize. In 2021, *Flèche* was a Lambda Literary Award Finalist. Chan won the 2018 Geoffrey Dearmer Prize and was shortlisted for the Forward Prize for Best Single Poem in 2017 and 2019, receiving an Eric Gregory Award in 2019. Chan's second book, *Bright Fear* (Faber, 2023), is a Guardian Best Poetry Book of 2023 and was shortlisted for the Forward Prize for Best Collection, the Writers' Prize and the International Dylan Thomas Prize.

WISH BEAR

Jo Bratten

Who's that coming from somewhere up in the sky
Moving fast and bright as a firefly?
—Care Bears Countdown

We're in the car at the mall and my mother
is crying because I have spent all my money
on a Care Bear the colour of soap.

A star falls from its tummy, smiling.
My new brother cries also, in the back.
He is probably hungry. His hands are ugly

pink claws. My father has not had new
jeans for two years she says. I think rain
falls. She doesn't mention the cancer

but it sits between us in the cold like
recrimination, with the powdered milk,
stale tostadas and Little Debbie cakes

that dad brings home from supermarket
dumpsters. Wish Bear smells clean and new.
I touch the hard little heart on its bottom

like a talisman, proof of its provenance,
Louboutin red. I will be transfigured
by its magic; the stars will smile for me.

In my bedroom the bear looks all wrong.
I become ashamed of it, the acerbic green,
its celluloid grin. It curses the house

with vermin: rat snakes nest in the eaves,
mice tumble through crumbling plaster.
My father's jeans are still full of holes.

When all the other stuffed toys rot in storage
Wish Bear remains intact, bright-eyed, its red
heart as hard as ever, its tummy trailing stars

like Lucifer hurled headlong flaming
from the ethereal sky, its tongue whispering
fraudulent temptation. Pluck, it says, eat.

SALOBREÑA

Tom Bailey

There were men smoking squid on sticks halfway down the beach.
It was one of those days when you think to yourself:
this could make a happy memory.
The sun was out at Salobreña. We were being kids again.
We smoked a spliff and chased each other
with seaweed in our hair.
We climbed the rocks and jumped into the sea,
though the reasons we climbed and jumped were complicated.
Memories must be carefully constructed, after all.
Look at the man rubbing sun-cream on the back of his wife's arms,
holding her body the way you'd hold a crystal.
Look at the children playing,
the kite sketching figures of eight in the sky.
Everything else is best let go of: how we heard all day
the thud of the knife
hacking fish heads off in the *chiringuito* kitchen;
how someone cut their foot on the rocks
and bled all the way up the hill to the bus station.
I love five people approximately and none of them are here.

THE CHILDREN HAVE FORGOTTEN TO BE AFRAID

Sarah Terkaoui

when another bomb lands
sends up great concrete splinters.
mushrooms the city.
they may pause,
speculate on where
the hit was, whether
there will still be school.
perhaps plan a new route
to their playgrounds
amongst burned out cars
street craters and
ruined apartment blocks
that turned into cemeteries.
they will not stop, flinch,
cry out. they cannot be
afraid of their lives.

EXACTLY AS MUCH

Olive Franklin

as a butterfly longs to tangle with the clean
dawn air   as a fallen earring seeks out
the dark openings of drains   as spaghetti turns weak
for boiling water   as plums nestle pits
as fingers anchor palms   as all small, dark
things that choose to hold each other
as fungi lash their roots together   as pebbles
smash each other to sand on the open beach

BURST ME INTO SONG
Isabelle Baafi

    although perhaps

                                          not a symphony

                              but a hum

perhaps aloe vera for ulcered gums

                          and leaf shadows dappling our chests

              perhaps the equinox

                      perhaps afrobeats

perhaps yams   perhaps

            homeostasis

        perhaps orange peel brightens dark

                              thoughts

      and the scar on my face

gives a lecture

        on beauty   perhaps you hand me a fig

          and our fingers graze

                    and we leave the roast chicken

to burn

       perhaps the chivalry of autocorrect   the motherhood

of bleach
          perhaps your dirty socks and my unread books

     the papercut   the sucked thumb   the blood

                            covenant

      perhaps the alarm   warns us

  about us

                perhaps

enough points for a free latte

     perhaps vegan steak   zero waste

the book of john

                  perhaps three buses in a row

perhaps the postman

     holds the lift

              and the safety pins

   are where we last saw them

Note: The title for this poem is borrowed from a line in 'The Virgin Speaks of What She Endured' by Shivanee Ramlochan.

PRAYING TO ÂU CO AFTER MY FIRST CERVICAL SCREENING

Natalie Linh Bolderston

Âu Cơ,
Today I pushed my fists under my hips
and said your name. My mother says
you were a mother before anyone else,
and so all our women can find you
at the salted edges of their flesh.
   Long ago, before I ever called on you,
a warm pain unravelled and I stopped
singing mid-hymn, convinced someone
would know. Another time, I left a stain
in a friend's bed, along with something
solid, like a boiled leaf.
   Âu Cơ, even now I only know you
by the wringing of your hands.
Sometimes, you are the woman
in my dreams, who bails out an ocean
using her daughter's hair,
births mountains when she feels the stars shift.
More often, you are the faint bird
my mother draws in the margins of letters.
   Âu Cơ, I should tell you
we still have our own ways of holding on
to our bodies, like the tea my mother swears
will nourish the womb and lead
to healthy pregnancy.
When asked, *does this hurt?*
we still lie, brace our knees,
stare into brittle white light.

[SOMETIMES I THINK I'M THE WRONG TYPE OF GAY]

Serge ψ Neptune

after James McDermott

sometimes i think   i'm the wrong   type of gay
not into   clubbing poppers   not insta
glam   enough   not gym rat enough
swiping   for a new encounter   pounded
in dark alleys   smelling of piss

sometimes the body grows   mythical
hydra-like   flicking pages   it differs from the hunks
in attitude   out   gay times   sometimes i overflow
with grief   chipped cup   leaking tub   what the mirror
reflects   what body   i inhabit   differ

i'm the wrong   type of gay   rugby players   fuck me bareback
in expensive rooms   at the bulgari the savoy   no such thing
as being old   i grow out   of myself
every seven years   carry   myself over
to the next man's   lips   a brazen vessel

a holy host   to melt   on the tongue   at the end
of his long day   sometimes   i think i'm the wrong
type of gay   at dawn   the river
drags   in its mournful wake   all the names
of men I loved   who fucked me   scarred me
or left me for dead   which is the same

GOOD IMMIGRANT

Yanita Georgieva

I recommend a city.
She says *not that city*.
I have heard bad things.
What things? *It's all*
falafel shops and foreigners.
You mean foreigners like
me. *No. Different.* In France
I am stopped at the border
by a woman who studies
my passport like a counterfeit
bill, a tenner I might use
to buy cigarettes. In class,
I am told to write more
about suffering,
to steal another tongue
for better sonics.
My family is happy
there are Balkan shops
on my street. The locals tell me
things have changed here.
No one at home will believe
what they call us, how worried they are
we might stay –
except my grandfather
who asks *and how do they see you*
then every summer
asks me again.

ACCORDING TO MARTIN
Simon Maddrell

i love to sit on that garden bench
                the one made out of recycled cartwheels
the way i feel about myself
                   how i wonder about my sibling
                 sculpted from rock
i blend camaraderie & outrage
      like starlings & squirrels
                   though both are fringed
                   with grey & regret
the way basil turns bitter-sweet
                   if cut by a knife
how sometimes sweetness can only be smelt
                   by ripping things apart
how often i'm torn between
                tongue & belly
                   pink & blue textures
         ice cream & cum
the way a spider spins silk   & eats its prey
    he loves to imagine
        what lies beneath it & who
              am i   playing in this drama
         which character   singing what

THERE IS NO BELIEF WITHOUT UNBELIEF
Sanah Ahsan

the qibla points me to a shin-sized
bin against a wall

a brown-spotted banana tongue is
spilling from repletion and

a blood clot the size of a goldfish
passes between my legs still

i kneel bare-headed & unwudud at
the janamaz three hours late for fajr auditioning for

approval from my god who hasn't
washed between their toes in days

the unbelief is swelling in my belly
i pray it is stillborn but it rushes out with ten

tiny fingers and ten tinier toes
wailing with holy life

god scoops it up rocking until
our terror becomes the melody we both sing

ISSUE TWO

November 2022
Edited by Jeremy Noel-Tod

JEREMY NOEL-TOD teaches in the School of Literature, Drama and Creative Writing at the University of East Anglia and was the *Sunday Times* poetry critic from 2013 to 2021. He is the editor of *The Penguin Book of the Prose Poem* (2018), the *Complete Poems of RF Langley* (2015), and *The Oxford Companion to Modern Poetry* (2013).

FROM WORK POEMS: 10

Charlotte Geater

crystals of the cave   fire at home,
Antigone   in the new body of her dishwasher
washing machine   a late-in-the-day
playdate   boosts
     your self-esteem
leaving earth for Orion / an onion
     a 'sumptuous' debut
after an IT glitch   up your arm glitters
retires   a city of friends
a library of bathroom stalls
with lowered doors   this fresh content
affects me   /   and doesn't affect me
in my reservations   and photo permissions

INEVITABILITIES

Oluwaseun Olayiwola

'Well, of course: who wants to be born?'
—Hannah Sullivan, Three Poems

and having been castaway (different
to being thrown
out of the light) by a wind

though what truly these days
is the difference when the body
is, law-like, always involved, when

the scatteredness grief
makes of devotion lies before you
like a stupid adjective rolling

the grass: inevitable
is the way any swinging thing
finds rest: (as in what we ought

to do after being fought
into parenthood; what
we leave behind) at the bottom—

the helicopter's aftermath
a violent fire-dream hollowing
out the seen through to space behind

the eyes
like a tattoo. My mother
forbade us to bring

any permanent mark
to our skin—son;
ever-unfolding crack

in the wall. My mother
had dreams, I think,
with grace and aplomb

is how I stole them—

MEN'S TOILET HAIKU
Jackson Phoenix Nash

Flushing, wait for them
to leave, boys who might see through
your clothes, your beard, you.

DEAD FOX
Dide

I saw a dead fox in the road today, in between the coming and going lanes, how a lady of the house would find the sickness of their cleaner an inconvenience. The roadkill had been lustre and bushy-fluffed, with a healthy red glow worthy of taxidermy when I had cycled past fresh in the morning. Now a few hours later, I couldn't look. It had reduced in size like good boiled sauce, and had crimson tendrils flaying off in Expressionist lines. Mangled and diminished, the forced puberty from girl to woman, an opportunity lost, how through all the chores and chores some don't enjoy the home/life, exhausted when night-time knocks for its ferry fare.

TEACH JACKDAWS AVIONICS

Taz Rahman

The sun does not fuss, days survive, clematis curates purple
in alleyways for blackbirds to core arcs in hunger, sing

to flowers, discourse evenings stretched on grass. Fingers
frack surfaces, erupt touch, catch aphids, time, molten

cores, questions — questions like why is the asphodel so
hardy in its narrow grass-like leaves, the stem elongating

the handsomest spike in white so unheard lives may
meadow in its six flirting petals. The sun hides in roof-lines

past noon, enters fan vaults warming chimneys to seduce
the fattest pigeon lit like silty grains carrying miles. May

bees shake their own cowbells, vine inquisition into mahonia
blooming too early in inclines no right to smile, a kingdom of

floating purr climbs a wall, wags tail like another species, in
the field nearby goats cough, neigh soft, thud hooves, pretend

to be stallions feeding a chorus of want wanting to stir, morning
chairs touch napes of human arms inside a high street café, pine

flesh, the leftover rose, its wilting stem aching to sit upright, trace
the night gone, one last glance at something to trail lost snails.

AT BARROW HILL

Natalie Burdett

I am not in awe
of the galvanised cross –
shining tall though scratched,
graffiti paint clotting
at welding joints.

Geological forces
are much less wary-making
than two men
scrambling through ivy
unbalanced by heavy rucksacks.

Miners cleared out graves
to get to limestone,
and weathering left
igneous dolerite proud,
resistant to dropped chip forks.

On a downhill path
I pick late blackberries
but a lone man
sidles into trees,
disappears as a front approaches.

Near to the estate,
the quiet comfort
of a million pale leaves
touching the faces of
those closest to them, very gently.

OVER THE BONES OF THE DEAD

Alex Jenkins

Coulters split the land's curdled
belly till the bones
      disclosed redged
unseeded furrows, edges
burred; ard blades notched
      like vertebrae

Farmers plotted
according to death
      crops feasted on bone
marrow; barley was sown in eye
sockets, oats in the sciatic notch
      Roots bedded in stromal
cells; ligules forced
foramina. Harvest after

      harvest
      grains swelled
to apostrophes

Worm tongues forgive
the plough's harrowing
symmetrical draft

The dead are practised speakers

who enunciate through buckled
rock sucked smooth
in the mouth's rockery

who mill flour to be laved and shaped
to bake consonants in the crust,
vowels in the crumb

who breathe spells through steam
curling from each torn farl.

RADISH MONODY

Ben Philipps

In the ache of summer a pigeon descends probably.
Another making of the sun. An air like resin.
In the ache of resin the pigeon seeks another air,
seeks it lower than the sun. A specific air is hot gel searing
on skin, on nape. How licit gleams the stucco;
how expert its seeming warp. Talbot now. The sky is paltry phrase.
One day, his father brought home a wave.
A small one, no real plunge, but he carried it,
furtive, in a damp pocket for us. Talking point. It glints still
unbreaking on the fireplace. So holocenes can't but be punctual
even if the old jokes don't ring true. And there is immobility
in principle, too, but still the pigeon traces lower. It droops,
he thinks, and knows drowsily, knows probably
there's no way at all from an exact furnace.
If at night the radish dreams. What will suffice.

RELATIONSHIP AS COVERED RESERVOIR

Paul Stephenson

All the years close to water. By a bulk of water. That hulk of water. Flat water. Still water. Being water. Water in the dark. Oblivious water. Obviously water. Water where water should be. Water with a roof. With walls. A body of water. Shared water. Everyone's water. Neighbouring water. Neighbourly water. Water with grass on. You couldn't walk on. Water close by. Closed off water. Water behind railings. Water off limits. Supposed water. Ought to be water. Take your word for it water. Water under lock and key. Padlocked water. Water with Keep Out signs. Official water. Officious water. Measured water. Metred water. Believed in water. Believed to be water. Hypothetical water. Water waiting. Patient water. Water biding its time. Well-behaved water. Weekday water. Rainy day water. Rained on water. Going nowhere water. Water treading water. Water concealed. Unrevealed. Knew no surprise water. No twilight, sunrise water. No boats or swans water. Nothing floating water. No running on water. Water not sailed on. No kid's laughing water. Water you could land a helicopter on. Take off from. Drown a city with water. Water we presumed to be water. Took for granted water. Ignored for years water. Didn't think twice about water. Blind to water. Could have broken into water. Jumped up and down on water. Hard water. Difficult water. By itself water. A watery self. Water alone. Lonely water. Encased water. With a lid on water. Couldn't breathe water. Or evaporate water. Let off steam water. Dry water. Shy water. Reserved water. Quiet water. Some days not speaking water. Water working. Water not working. Getting worked up water. Water we ran and ran.

I

Irum Fazal

I hold still snow by fig and olive
recursion never looked so good
Jerusalem and Laundress Lane stumbled
the sweetest cold projection, cease

and this safe city mulberry static
Then reduced them to the lowest of all
And it is my belief that all, that almost all, if not all pathologies
stem from complexity

the soothing, poorest visibility. barefoot, retreat
detained in an airport.
Who knows what you ever meant, deleted and new
fingerprints, vicious trees and dissolving warmth:
if I breathe you could be gone for good.

ISSUE THREE

January 2023
Edited by Rebecca Tamás

REBECCA TAMÁS is the author of the poetry collection *WITCH* (Penned in the Margins, 2019), which was a Poetry Society Choice and a Paris Review Staff Pick. Rebecca's essay collection *Strangers: Essays on the Human and Nonhuman* (Makina Books, 2020); was longlisted for the Rathbones Folio Prize 2021. She is a Lecturer in Creative Writing at City University, London.

NATAL NOISES, FATAL FLAWS
Muskaan Razdan

I took my mother's tooth, I needed bones. She pushed me
a month early, she needed joy. An understanding
to take what's needed without asking, without needing to,
even before birth. Crouched on a couch, she crochets
veins to protect me. I become hope, before a body. Fattening her
heart with promise. A foetus learns language in the womb. Silence
meant rage. Piercing my placenta, forming cysts of suppression.
I replied with itches against sheer skin. She soothed me. Clawing herself,
creating upward trails. She said, for you I'll pray
                      (Amniotic fluid reverbs her voice)
                                I learned,
                                          for you I'll prey.

EN PLEIN AIR

Clíodhna Bhreatnach

Peach clouds & furze in my field of vision;
the cliffs, the gulls, Kinsale! Who frescoed this sky
with weekend, blushing perfectly, & I would die
for this green green grass —
              would it die for me?
See how my heart is like a swimming pool —
how cool a splash each look at something beautiful —
  even the private golf course can't
  colonise the view, so I turn to look:
my tiny friends against the static blue;
my boyfriend stooping in the purple dulse;
over him humped cliffs of golden barley;
how enormously orange the sun convulses
to a sliver of itself, & how night is so clear
I become a pure eyeball for the constellations
& the moon's cream gulp. No dreams of emails
come tonight. No floating text, no faces bleared
by blue light & thumb. In the morning the sun
sears Saturday to earth. A small black crab
      sidles out of sand to eat my boyfriend's
feet, as onto knuckles, onto lap,
      onto blanket, onto sand, a whitely
dripping ice-cream. No clouds, only sky;
a pink burn amalgamates the freckles
on my boyfriend's neck and my eye turns crystal
out of joy at all these vivid totalities,
such as this blue unbroken sea of no armadas
today, but maybe tomorrow, & glittering,
like a diamond that cuts the calendar open.

AL-ASRAR

Ali Fitzpatrick

Parked in the middle of my street, anchored
by your citadel, distant, bathed in light,
we removed our sallowed skins unhampered
and kissed with breath inflected by finite
touches and teases and remnants of gin,
of rizlas gracing the edge of a tongue,
of hairs dusting pathways from ear to chin.
I'd have offered you myself to be wrung
out and consumed - devoured even - 'til
I remembered the calm of me, herself,
a curious constant renewed of will,
un-haloed but hallowed, crowned without wealth.
And so, as two forms, distinct, we parted,
a more intricate weave than when we started.

POEM BEGINNING WITH A LINE BY AR AMMONS

Caspar Bryant

Since words were introduced, Things have gone poorly for the planet
Rivers and oceans met each other and did not mix. So too stars, which
discovered they weren't each other. Entirely.
Beetles played monopoly with the biggest landlords *and won* with their
400,000 described species, metamorphic pupal stages, and their
trillions of forenames, surnames, middle names, and marital names.
Things piled up in crab-buckets and dictionaries. You were found listed
under *distant*. I have more or less money now.
All one breath broke and distributed itself across pairs, triplets, the real
absence of lungs. I wrote less.

The butterfly population boomed, throwing millions of flower species
into hyperpollination.
Colours grew complicated and took longer to think about. They sound
Like runaway marbles on cobbled streets. You blinked twice
And found a name for everything, ran from the station shouting *TAXI*,
shouting
DRIVE, shouting *MIDDLE-CLASS CONCESSION TO
CONVENIENCE*. At the beach howling
PLASTIC PLASTIC and *PLASTIC GARBAGE* at the Ammonite, you
give in, you crawl in,
Humming in the shell-walls shouting *SEA*.

THE FROG WIFE

Livia Franchini

After Millhauser

Like peeling back a poinsettia blossom
or a concept of iceberg proportions

Language can be thick with flesh both
that; & very deep & very cold

A sugary rope, same taste
in the teeth as pink mouse

Somebody's babies
They cross the street and you let them walk on

Once they make it to the other side
you spin around looking for their parents

The children disappear from view
And you've lost your train of thought

Chewing on the long beard of language
its granular bristle full of Os

It is a strange city you live in
buildings as grey as Dumbo
& before you know

You are a burning hot dot
And you have forgotten to take your son home

HOW TO LEAVE
Ciara Maguire

worry, often; keep a glass of milk next to the bed for when she gets home; find yourself lying in flowerbeds for a moment of relief; realise that water is always shifting; sleep on the floor when it all gets too much; walk across the city at 5am when it is still too much; lock the bathroom door for a moment of relief; arrive to work an hour early and leave an hour late; realise you can catch the sunrise this way; realise there are worse places to watch it than from the fourth floor of an office building; go numb every morning; make a game of burning your own arm to check you can still feel; watch the infected burns turn the same yellow as the sunrise; go to a nightclub and find a corner to sleep in; kiss someone else; tell yourself it was a mistake; do it again; drive out of the city; keep going; say nothing; seek out crosses; seek out images of god; seek out objects of protection; let her win; let her lose; try to find meaning in any of it; notice the cat has pissed in her trainers and say nothing; absorb the yelling; become a conduit; wash her trainers; create a narrative in which this is your one great love; keep your eyes shut; let her face become anyone else; when autumn comes cut your hair off; feel a renewal; when winter comes remind yourself you could leave; don't; let her grip on your arm tighten; let words fall out of your head; become a fridge; slowly defrost; watch the world glow orange; take a pill & fight the first man you see; leave your shoes in the street; find beauty in a small town church hall; start a fire; put it out; what did you expect; let the sky unfold; let blood fall out of you in strange clumps; ask your friends, is this normal; ignore the responses; become plankton; float idly through each day touching nothing; touch is where the trouble starts; become a moving target; let yourself be hit; rearrange your own reality; run; let the milk go sour; never follow through; spend a week on the floor with someone else; anyone else; keep running; become the sun; leave

IN THE DISTANCES OF THIS COUNTRY

Rojbîn Arjen Yiğit

my moon is tomorrow
time is three hours
in difference
now we sleep
in the others' zone
I am in between language
amphibious and tongueless
I only just want to
complicate you
heat you like an agnostic
it is hard to not have faith
at the breast of a fig tree
my ears clamped down to
the pillow
tell a whisper
a small something
self-persuasion of you
loving me
talk to me hostile
about Istanbul
lick the buzz off my skin
sweating red
my canines on your
ear and any lobe you fancy
the sun comprehending glass
hours after we have come ourselves
flitting sharp january angles
moaning out for the fig tree
o the distances of this wretched country

WAREHOUSE

Tom McLaughlin

for Derek Jarman

To sleep inside
a greenhouse in
the centre of
an empty space
while the river
flings its patterns
on the ceiling
is to lean your
body against
the brickwork of
the suburban
bedroom that housed
your teenage years
until you feel
a wall give way

To fuck behind
a pane of glass
with a stranger
or a friend while
raised high on a
wooden platform
while the midday
sun douses you
in piercing light
somewhat dims the
memory of
nuns who always
came at night to
interrupt *the
lovely feeling*

Glass walls hold me
with such grace that
when the phone rings —
febrile in the
morning halflight
radiating
in waves of pain —
I do not think
but plunge my hand
clean through the glass
and hear the sound
of my childhood
crash around me
in fragments that
lodge in my skin

انار

Mohammad S. Razai

The autumn stretched like our neighbours' smokestacks into the choked sky dotted with clipped feverish kites. It was that time when the smell of burnt oak tingled the noses in Kabul, scratched the hatted heads and hacking chests shook the lanterns. You coughed your lungs out as the leaves kept falling silently wraith-like. One late afternoon we passed by the bared birches along the uni street, the field grown tense from piles of auburn, crimson, feuille morte. I almost lost you — dazzled by the old vendor's pomegranates, انار their lambency and lusciousness — among the pale violet burqas, I kissed your gnarled hands, your ringed finger brushed against my lip all but tearing my open mouth.

LOVE WHITE HOT LIKE GOD WHITE HOT LIKE GRIEF WHITE

Shayna Kowalczyk

two wholenesses plump and impenetrable.
my skin is thick as grapefruit, warming pockmarked
in the winter sun. her head bobs sweetly. am I
unmoved? I think idly of rupturing & scorching the earth.
'how do well-adjusted people fall in love?'
I google, 'how do securely attached people
fall in love?' but there is no initiation. newly,
I am as mellow as duck feathers: as soft, as kind.

I discovered love as
revelation: the urgent baring of things. soon, I was
targeting pliable hearts in ragged confessionals
on the midnight curb side. I, a lightning rod of shock
& raw feeling. love, like pouring. love, like
I am an emptying vessel and here floods every terrible thing
I have ever felt and you, innocently, have never known to feel
you are welcome / receive me / save me / receive me

she stretches languidly. healed,
I am studiously disinterested in violence. I gaze
at my woollen gloves, the vacant skyline.
I used to be fortressed & vulnerable; now I walk unconcealed,
wholly untouchable. there is no electricity in the
honest confusion of being alive. our arms swing
childishly. I close my eyes. there must be a way
of learning to love her without first
destroying myself at her feet.

ISSUE FOUR

March 2023
Edited by Jack Underwood

JACK UNDERWOOD is a poet, writer and critic. He author of *Happiness* (Faber, 2015), *Solo for Mascha Voice* (Test Centre, 2018) and *A Year in the New Life* (Faber, 2021). His debut work of non-fiction, *NOT EVEN THIS*, was published by Corsair in 2021, exploring parallels between quantum physics, black hole science, cyborgism, and the philosophies of language and knowledge and poetics, all through the lens of new parenthood. He has collaborated widely with composers and artists, and his work has been published internationally and in translation. He is co-presenter and curator of the Faber Poetry Podcast and is a senior lecturer in Creative Writing at Goldsmiths College, and is currently working on a collection of short fiction.

AUGURY

Miruna Fulgeanu

Girl with juniper mouth,
I am only beginning

to begin the dream from
which like a lamp

you walk me out.
It's been twenty bad years,

spent fleeing
the feeling that I

might be about to hear you
asking for my kindness.

And what am I to do
now with this

hand you give me, rifle-like,
conspicuous, the hand

of a girl not-drowning? I
must put in my love

hours, graceless,
and walk. All around,

the fragrant thicket
darkens & hums.

WHAT I HEAR WHEN SISTERS COMPARE UPBRINGINGS

Kayla Marie Troy

    the scene started with an anthem the scene started with a warm summer room and torsos of desk wood home to the worn names of fidgeting girls who watch boys and boys who with a silk insult drop elbows in class mid-song

    some girls mime word for word while dem teachers curl pretty as de lip of a gun when that sound come on sis together they aspired to burn our schools down with dey mighty foreign tune pushin tru

    god save the something some ting god save this country together we are the country it's in our throats but sis I never sang it much I was just a body of mum's hail mary's at the time yet you were seventeen trading island for island

    I know I wasn't born but was still singing with you at the dock sis you hung from a rosary our nation bird arung yuh neck tight so tight we sang mum's rhyme that loud it made us cry god save

    the sinking the ship the captain god save the servant the kitchen the floor the orchestra of bones the truck loads of adolescents who find life cropped at the heart its dimensions swinging the foot of the boat her hum hearing us fade

SEMI-ERMINE

Richard O'Brien

The stoats are getting all fucked up.
A nervous slice of marble cake,
a bad split bet zigzags across
the snow that didn't fall this year,

gone long enough for genes to make
their own cold calculation. Our mistakes
spring up before their time: red blooms
in winter, systems out of tune.

It's come to this – we didn't think –
or thought had nowhere it could go
except into compactor cubes
which slowly stack beneath the snow

that hasn't fallen yet, but will.
Prod, like an awkward attic hatch,
the great piñata of the clouds:
the ceiling is unsealing now,

containment breached, ready to spill
on stoats, on grass, on moss, on mud,
on bulbs, on buds, on them, on us,
on television, there in black and white.

CODEX DREAM

Lucie Richter-Mahr

You're asleep
in a forest
of blue trees
You're lying down
inside a clearing
I'm there, in the circle,
watching you sleep
but
I'm also
somewhere
colder
I'm closing
and opening my eyes
inside a cloud
I'm on top of
a mountain
trying
to tell you
some urgent piece
of news — that *death
has no terrors*
but it does have,
for instance,
a lion
walking slowly
through the forest
of blue trees

Now I'm in a petrol station
where you buy me
a packet
of Polos
It's been years
since my last
Polo!
Your palm
is a bright
spark
beneath the LED
& further out
the horizon
rumbles
Headlights
fill up
the lower
fractus clouds
*No essence can exist without
its concrete being*,
so, yes —
I'm on the asphalt
But I'm also
walking

backwards into
a cool ring
of stars
Behind
the building
Over
the road
Into
a field of cornflowers
Yes,
I'm watching
from behind
the blue trees
while a lion
without features
comes slowly,
softly,
to eat
a shining
Polo
from your hand

THE REMAINS OF SKY
Memoona Zahid

'You remember too much, / my mother said to me recently. / Why hold onto all that? And I said, / Where can I put it down?'"
        — Anne Carson, Glass, Irony and God

the night when I thumbed the spine of our photo album
Pari said   *I don't recognise anyone in there*
I try to forget   I try the goodhonesthard way
keep my eyes down   spill buttercups from my mouth
     I've been swallowing magic
tricks and laughing my insides
         out
   I carry tangerines in my backpack
crushed at the bottom   I carry my first name which mama
forgot to put on my birth certificate
         what's in a name Pari says
I carry a lock of my own hair I carry the smell of sweat and sleep
and longing I carry sediment from my solar plexus
         crushed at the bottom
   let go of all that Pari says
and lets her smile curl into the palm of my hand like the sun newly
opening itself
   as she dredges weeds from my corners but I simmer I dig
my heels into this ground
     as thousands of pigeons halt   in the remains of sky
not a flutter or a gentle swoop
      just the thud   of a hawthorn tree chopped

FOREIGN BODIES
Iulia David

Dousing my long hair in gasoline to kill lice, Mama,
you make me into a delicate flame waiting to happen.

I breathe once and my scalp, twice a blessing of your
hands, opens into a humble suburban road. Ask me

where I am going as I am closing my eyes and I say
here's a street lamp, with its unlidded eye, here's a hole

in the dark – on the way to school, I am the only familiar
planet. If my body was all ears, I could hear people eating

their bread in dreams, I could catch the frogs spawning
when I hop the ditch to escape a man with a match

for a mouth striding behind my back – he is stroking it,
stroking the match to light the match – between me

and him a dead-end word, *cunt* – if only the freckles on my
knuckles could guide me like stars, if only the road would fork

or I would cross but the traffic in your lap is crazy, Mama –
this must be how water felt when it turned into wine

and this is how it rises above the ankles in the bath
as you are rinsing my blonde hair, two fistfuls of gold

on a blue towel, me – landing in my body like a ship looking
for a new home, you – counting my luck, strand by strand,

each unextraordinary ringlet a kind of knowing
how the morning sky could have gone both ways.

ABSeas

Martha Aroha Челок

*'and i was already on my way to being a true freak because i knew i
would always choose to go where my blood beats: in any and all directions'*
— bell hooks

the first complex organism in the world was Algaeic,
anaerobic amoebae
in Blood, the elements sodium, potassium, and calcium combine in
roughly the same proportions as sea water
one day, a group of Cells aggregated into a slug-like mass
now look at you
look at how you are scribbling
when before you was just scratching the surface
another hypothesis: when the first organism divided, the Daughter
cells failed to separate, resulting in a conglomeration of identical cells
in one multicellular organism, people
who would yield to the first softness in a mute and absurd cosmos
cheek-to-cheek with sedimented rock,
life is just a dud
in the water (daughter),
carry the pail of it

LITTLE IRONIES
Jared Collins

It's not just recalling something otherwise lost.
It's not even remembering what's there to remember.
It's running your cold hand under colder water and
making notes about what kind eyes your reflection has.
I'm not saying you will have kindness there, but
just noticing is kindness,
and either way the water bill can't run as high
as your hormones at sixteen, or your friend or father's
legs could help them jump... I've been noticing
little ironies in your speech lately, like 'It's not about
recalling something lost, it's just finding your way
through a corn field on an overcast night' –
Too many ears and stalks to touch them all, yet making way
for carrion by morning. See, it's not the wind that finds you
it's you that finds the wind.

                                     Oh. Pain in a dream is just like
dental work. You get the crumbs of agony here and there
but on the other end will thank your loose memory –
Looser still than a blackberry rotting on its stem, or better yet,
cockles at the end of their tenancy. When each bud is squeezed
you take in new flavours, might just tighten your thumb
around the punctured thorn – new fuel mixing with new fuel.

CAPACITY

Rebecca McCutcheon

T drives me to the coast for work, a black sky
feigns oblivion. I've been starving for months
done the stuff films tell you not to. There's less
of me to worry about. I once got so wet
nothing could help. Everything is closed;
off-season, empty like a spent hen.
I follow the road until it becomes a sea
straight-lining so I don't get lost. I'm not
sure how I'm getting through these nights.
The hamster is excavating its bed while I text
strangers. I can't sleep; he sweats in the alley
like a stray. She's a cheaper lover than I am
if she only writes you acrostic poems. T thinks
we'd make great travelling salesmen, glitters
when she tries it. I don't know how to be angry
except for those last two times. *I think we're going
to need another bottle*. I grieve old love on the glass
and the room like a mouth falls down.

LIKE A CHILD IN A STORY BOOK

Rachel Curzon

I remember it was late summer. I had slept and missed the months of June, July and August. Nobody had touched my shoulder or shaken me awake. Knowing that this would have been my role in other circumstances and knowing that I would have performed it well, I was bitter. Yes, I can say this here. I came stiffly into a room where everyone was talking and they turned so casually to look. I went for a walk. The door was open; the view was inviting in the way a painting of a garden gate invites, or the small space between a garage and a fence. I followed the path without wondering where it led. I remember rubbing my eyes, like a child in a story book. When the road branched I did not hesitate but took the left fork, quite confidently. I passed a family with a picnic on a tartan rug; they tossed me a quail's egg and I have it even now in the side of my cheek, still whole. I did not want to leave the road. I definitely did not want to find a crawlspace between stones and spend a long night listening to owls in the branches. I had certainly meant to tell people of my whereabouts. I think at that stage I intended to return.

ISSUE FIVE

May 2023
Edited by Alycia Pirmohamed

ALYCIA PIRMOHAMED is the author of *Another Way to Split Water* (Polygon / Yes Yes Books, 2022), the pamphlets *Hinge* (Ignition Press, 2020) and *Faces that Fled the Wind* (BOAAT Press, 2019), and the collaborative work *Second Memory* (Guillemot Press, 2021), co-authored with Pratyusha. She is co-founder of the Scottish BPOC Writers Network, a co-organiser of the Ledbury Poetry Critics, and she currently teaches Creative Writing at the University of Cambridge. Alycia received an MFA from the University of Oregon and a PhD from the University of Edinburgh.

IMPALA

Caitlin Tina Jones

Do you sometimes see yourself in pictures and wonder
How you managed to stay alive, so unknowing
Of all the mangled eaves hushed over you,
Dangled soft in front of you, like a claw hammer and
A wish, playing in the mouth of the taped-off lane.
Ally had ridden down it
And I could see her caved-in head, a broken
Round vase, forbidden purpling and powdered glass
On the tarmac, and how my heart had pounded
What a normal thing it was to cry then, to cry and
Then to laugh, how they held my wrists and not my
Hands, to avoid my eyes and the rumour water.
But she'd cycled back, so safe, sculpted
Fresh and translucent in the summer, annealed and beaming
Saying it was fine, saying a man would never catch her
Too fast and far too bright, and I could see her as an impala then
And never anything else, sheer prongs stuttered golden in the light.

DREAMCATCHER
Zahra Rafiq

Pellucid in deception you thread
Your calculations together in silk
Stitches. Of every crevice in my room
You chose the ceiling of the windowsill
A fault line crossing realities. The sun is not
Destined to rise for another 4 hours
But I am awake and dressed
4:30am in my business suit. I don't think
You ever sleep, you're relentless in
Furnishing your silvery home with more
Silver, a diaphanous mirror raging
In your puddle of dark. It fascinates me
A load bearing biomaterial stronger
Than steel. I want to be a bullet when I smile,
Lethal and promising and fast.
You weave them together in a sort
Of tapestry, your way of justifying your future
With tragedies. As if to remind me
You're not the villain in this story.
Remember my blonde tresses, how they turned
To gossamer with ammonia persulfate –
There was no saviour here.
Suddenly you've stopped and you're silent.
I begin to mourn, but then
Eight obsidian needles climb the web
Swallow the shooting star whole.

WHAT SHOULD WE DO WITH OUR SUPERSTITIOUS FATHERS

Lucille Mona Ling

unlearned love crawls

        into their arms,   children

Not us

                                    others,
                                    self-made or

left

            in the cribs of water lilies

      e*astern* statues of stars

embedded in the octagonal petal dress

                        they wear bracelets around their wrists

Don't let me continue

Don't let me continue

                            you'd rather I erase these

symbols of fractal misinterpretation

        the red crying

                the infinite yellow   wishes for better roofs

      I have seen your hands dance

To music

Loud in the shell of the metallic

car

care

                        taker
Takeaway the t

                                    and you leave the puppet
Aching

                                                achieving inanimate emotions
                                                            known to AI
ai
            to love

aime
love me
                                there are so many languages ai
Can learn

                                                                            I
Can learn
                                to aimlessly improvise healing
The tea leaves that predicted
                                            green misfortunes have now rotten into

Auspiciousness,
            I remember how you listened
To hypnotic
To repetitive
Music inaccessible
                                    to small ears
Too hypnotic
Too repetitive

                        too small
                                                too childish
Listen to the outside,   beyond

the rhythm lie

            goosebumps:
                                    hills of transcen

dance

Notes:

1. *Stern* means 'star' in German.
2. *Ai* means 'love' in Chinese.
3. *J'aime* means 'I love' in French

CHOOSING JEWELS

Francesca Brooks

I like the slick lacquered lid
      of a mushroom in the damp,
  shy
of the secret of its gills
              vaulted, ticklish,
     a kind of velvet
intended only to be known
         by leaf rot   forest floor.

The swamps are ferrous,
       moss-edged   fogged with spore

I stay close
      to the waxy fluorescence
of Orange Peel ascocarps,
         the snuffed wicks
     of the Candlestick fungus
like the small,
      pale arm that reaches
from a wet log

I dream of the ice caves of
       Bearded Tooth   Lion's Mane
mycelial snow cascade

find ears of jelly cupped to felled elder
      plush, evanescent,
         a maroon light listening

for parakeets   bark of heron disturbed,
a landscape
            intimate
      as the ridge of skin and cartilage
known only
            to pillow   lover's soft eye.

TOPSOIL

Shakeema Edwards

It's legal now in New York to compost bodies—
to return each atom to the earth
on beds of sawdust and alfalfa,
where microbes, fertile with purpose,
unravel them to the bone,

make them silt, clay, peat, or loam;
they will nourish beetles and worms,
hibiscus, bougainvillea, royal poinciana;
they'll regrow forests of sequoias
and cherry blossoms; they will flourish

and perhaps discover how God decided
which millipede would receive ocelli
and which, eyeless, would bioluminesce
beneath soil, unable to perceive
in the damp dark its own brilliance.

BITCH RIVER

Ellora Sutton

My body is a river in recovery from another body.
We're all just out here trying our best
but some people's best is fucking awful
and that's not my fault. I'm exhausted.
The sun cannot set in the same river twice
or something. I adore how its pink flesh pollutes
the river's mummy-flesh, like that time
on holiday, as a kid, when I was so sick
all that came up was rot and algae, bile and silt,
silt, the dark rind of a dagger so eroded
it was a mistranslation, a misunderstanding,
the slit in my side. Is my body property?
Help me, I need to change all the batteries
in all the smoke alarms and chandeliers,
the realtors are coming, I don't want them to notice
the water damage, the low ground,
the predictability of living
on a floodplain.

TURLOUGH

David Nash

Water with its moon in Libra:
now you see it,

sudden water, where yesterday
you'd happened

on a desire path
home, which would have halved

the time it takes. Now with water,
doubled. Doubled water –

the lake you see before you now is
the lake you don't

inverted, the water table
with its legs in the air,

an underground overed,
a frown upside-downed.

You roll up your jeans
to ford or afford it, and exactly at waist

height you are one of two things:
an anchor tethering sky

or the lake's space programme.
This water one day

will leave land in its wake.
You will stand in

a grass meniscus
while the water, untroubled,

summers in closure.
Now you don't.

SIREN
Karan Chambers

here is the night on a pen nib. sabre carved & starkened. cross-hatched stretch of stars. abyss. full. of not knowing. of teetering. here is the moon's bright arch. curving. guttural. coffee-stain ring of half. remembrance. here is marshland pressing. below a dead-rimmed sky. scalding. rabbit-eared tuft. of longing. bless me. for i have. desired. snatched. wanted. greedy-handed. stuffed my mouth so full. i choked. forgot myself. fleeting. here is the world in an ink spill. thickblack. gleaming. spread like faded light. painful. here the water. waits. eager. manuscript of anticipatory. silence. stuck. in soft-drift splendour. it's been years. since last i stood. here. straining. forwards motion. less. here are my fingers. exposed to the air. freezing. startled. by the depths. of not-being. here is the sound. of stiff-limbed. resignation. knotted. curling upwards. these are follies. delusions. half. snarled. roots of forgetting. wisped. vaporous. & somewhere. in the   not-here. a small word. of recognition.

SONNET (WITH AN UNTRANSLATED COPY OF FRAGOLETTA)

VJ René

Along the lilac lake, the lingering evening
Relinquishing the slight, soft fragrance of dying
Strawberry leaves, I thought of you sadly again

And all at once I was speaking in the language
Of a vague emphatic past, familiar to me
Only in reproduction, a tongue of anther

And of winglet. This is the unself-consciousness
Of pollen. This blue-black smear is the nightingale
The night breathes into its hands. These are the letters
Left in sand by a pair of snakes. This is the sea.

This is the sound of the strange scent of perfecting.
This is the moment in which they give you something
For the pain. And this is the moment in which you
Hold onto my hand and tell me it is hurting.

MORNING
Aleja Taddesse

makes a bad thing sing
makes a bad thing serenade suffering
mourning, slurring, feeding and tweeting under a brief blue sky
fumes and snuffed beams from night drives,
linger in patterns
sequences of stop-start sleep

morning brings a million revolutions a minute—
we are working, pedalling through
not as radical, resolute, as morning news presumes
morning—

a

released   kite

silk skirt on   cocoa-buttered
                                    skin.

morning, kin, morning friend, morning bossman!

who we praying for this morning?
where to cast our morning paper?
morning beautiful, fervent fodder

morning, let us now sing.

ISSUE SIX

July 2023
Edited by Karen McCarthy Woolf

KAREN MCCARTHY WOOLF: Born in London to English and Jamaican parents, Karen McCarthy Woolf FRSL is the author of two poetry collections and the editor of seven literary anthologies. Shortlisted for the Forward Felix Dennis and Jerwood Prizes, her debut *An Aviary of Small Birds* tells the story of losing a son in childbirth and was an Observer Book of the Year. Her latest, *Seasonal Disturbances*, explores gentrification, the city and the sacred, was a winner in the inaugural Laurel Prize for ecological poetry and excerpted in the Financial Times and the Guardian. In 2019 she moved to Los Angeles as a Fulbright Postdoctoral Scholar and Writer in Residence at the Promise Institute for Human Rights at UCLA, exploring the relationship between poetry, law and capitalism's impacts on black, brown and indigenous bodies.

She has presented and performed her work at literature festivals worldwide — in Mexico, Trinidad, Jamaica, Italy, America and China at a variety of venues such as the Royal Festival Hall, Barbican and King's Place for Poetica Electronica, which showcased music collaborations with various dance and techno producers. Her poems have been translated into Turkish, Swedish, Spanish, Polish and Dutch, produced as animated and choreographed short film, exhibited by Poems on the Underground and dropped from a helicopter over the Houses of Parliament in a poetry 'bombing'.

Karen also writes for radio and recent highlights include a multi-authored adaptation of Virginia Woolf's Orlando which was nominated for a BBC Audio Award in 2020 and a reversioning of Homer's Book of the Dead in which Odysseus is reimagined as a London cab driver for BBC Radio 4's Book of the Week. She has served as Chair and Judge of the Brunel International African Poetry Prize several times, was a judge of the National Poetry Competition in 2021 and is currently on the judging panel of the Forward Prize and Gingko Prize. After returning to the UK she travelled to Brazil in 2021 as an artist in residence at the Sacatar Institute in Bahia to research new work that explores sugar and its cultural and material legacies.

BEAT

Marina Scott

In memory of Brianna Ghey

what we have to do must be done in the now*
        now I might ask 'why is my city not cleaner'
we want to move beyond the beat of survival
        move faltering move across a line or border scramble to
beyond the beat of a beating of the bills of a weekday
        evening vigil for a child. what to do with this constant
grief, will you hold my grief, just for a moment, watch it fit the groove
        as in: a long, narrow cut or depression in a hard material.
through this hardening the polis polishes his horns
        pisses out legislation passing it like stone and
my parents browse electric cars accuse me
        of hyperbole when I use the word *fascist*
there are so many things to be thankful for
        the days growing
        fat and strong as
        concave truth fades
        in an empty room

*Audre Lorde

HOMESICKNESS
Elontra Hall

I take my nephew to a court I played on when I was his age. We talk about KD's crossover, physics homework and first kisses as clouds begin to pressure the sun. Detroit is not the same anymore, white people run barefoot in the street with their dogs off leash in neighbourhoods that would have made corpses of them only a few years earlier. Coming to the corner where a boy was shot selling weed last month, I tell my nephew to stop so I can scout ahead. This area has been 'rehabilitated' but I don't trust it. Oblivious, my nephew crosses the street, focused only on his dribble. Getting closer to the blacktop, he lobs me questions — *Hey Unc, why did you move away? Uncle Tré, do you ever miss anything about being here? Do you ever think of coming back?*

We arrive at the court, and the clouds hiss rain to drive us away. We look at each other, shrug and start to play anyway. I'm winning, enjoying this time with my kin when clouds break and I see him: aloft, ball a hairsbreadth from his fingertips as he ascends, rain plasters him like confetti, the light casts him in brass, and I turn my head to weep for what I've lost.

Between houses grass
sways. Bereaved and abandoned,
coyote pups howl.

WHO WE MOURN

Carson Wolfe

A contrapuntal written from words spoken in a documentary on The Yorkshire Ripper

there are a certain kind of women,	the ones that shock,
of loose morals, never from a	perfectly innocent
decent family. father distraught	a bright future taken
by the Jamaican boyfriend.	only sixteen, a young lass
streetwalking the red light.	so beautiful, such a waste.
very, you know,	worrying for the mothers,
frightening.	though a pretty death makes it easier.
within a respectable working class	no one wants
to look at dead whores	to dig a grave
is just too dark.	for the proper girls that live here.

LANDSCAPE WITH VAPOUR-SPRAYED AUBERGINES

Adam Heardman

In a gasp of mist
which seems to contain the sky,
vapour is induced onto fruit
outside organic chains.
The shifting of spring cloud
gives the impression of hours
passing over the ground
in patches, stripes. The striped
awnings, appetisingly
clownish, curve like tongues
away from the city brick,
a brick which echoes
a voice from somewhere,
resolving itself, after
a pulse, into the word
aubergines. So
you look at the aubergines,
tight dark balloons,
a confusion of orca-heads
breaching, wet with vapour
pulled from the sky, and look
at you, reflected as many
vague shadows in all
of the berries' domed foregrounds,
looming convexly, adding
several absences
shaped like persons

to the rubbery scene,
as if the solanine
and night-shaded fruit
were keeping you gone
from their spongy interiors.
Behind you in the world,
and before you as
a blank, swooped frame
in each slicked and bright-black
surface, the sky.

NEGATIVE CAPABILITY & THE TOMATOES
Claire Collison

All night I hear the rain drumming on the skylight in the bathroom, and it reminds me of the sound of my mum, peeing into a bedpan, and how we used to remark on that in the leather-sofa hospital surrounded by fields of tomatoes—how her peeing into the plastic bedpan sounded exactly like rain on the bathroom skylight at home. There's a bleary photo in the catalogue I bought in Almería, of a girl in Palomares eating a tomato from the time of the Incident—it's captioned 'Girl eating a Raf tomato'—which seems anachronistic; I don't think Raf tomatoes were a thing then. The point anyway was not what kind of tomato but how cavalier they were about the clean-up. I don't know if the tomatoes we ate were radioactive. Yesterday I went to a paint shop, to see if they'd any giveaway calendars, the ones with all the saint's days. They hadn't, but a man who'd been chatting to the woman on the till told me he'd one I could have. He took me to his gym nearby, explaining on the way that the calendar was from one of those companies that move earth—he gestured churning with his arms as he walked—and it was: I unrolled the calendar with its pin-up yellow JCB. The company was based in Palomares—where the bomb, where the tomatoes, where maybe the cancer. And it felt like a sign, these diggers chewing up the earth. And can I write about this if I don't have all the facts? Because that's not what I care about, the facts.

FINAL DESTINATION

Courtney Conrad

I remember learning how to write my name
while crossing the *Atlantic* on my mother's passport.
The British accent rooting itself without a naturalisation certificate.
I am one year shy of retirement when the six o'clock news notifies me
of the Home Office's shredder feeding on my landing card.

Two weeks later, thick envelopes make my letterbox retch—
eviction notices, NHS bills, and deportation warnings.
At work, my Line Manager leads two officers toward me,
one scoffs *'illegal'* like it's my first name.
The other announces *you are no longer allowed*

to work and live in this country. 'Mi wuk yah thirty years.
Pay mi taxes. Not even a bokkle of wata mi tief.'
This is the first time my colleagues hear me
speak Patois. Outside the office, breathless
my body lowers like a flag.

Paperwork muffles my family's wails.
The state calls me cargo and loads me onto a plane.
Within hours, I arrive in Jamaica, soil hungry.
The cemetery requires no papers for my residency.

THE BODY IS NOT AN APOLOGY
Titilayo Farukuoye

The body is not an apology
And yet I apologise.

    I step outward
step back ward
    I then duck,
        lean away.

slide
    pull in my belly
Pull in from behind
        step on my toes
    Duck again.

My body is not an apology
and yet
    It's the only thing
I've taught it to do.

CHIPPED SOUND

Mark Saunders

reading aloud to me   was like   early speech   emulators I
remember   as a teenager copying   strings of characters and phrases
the computer could speak   inhumanly   in strangely accented
letters   to impress my friends   saying the
words   how clever it was

sometimes   I would experiment with   unnatural clusters   sessions
of beatbox consonants   without vowels   clipped and guttural
typing in dk dp gk bp and hitting enter   for kick drums   and
a triggered snare   tchk   could be rolled over tchkchkchk
although the high frequency   phonemes screamed   metallic to
me resembling a crash   tssshh   or ride cymbal   tss   or a sequence
dp ch gkg ts stuck in a loop

I couldn't work out   if the spaces   translated into
measure   or time in any   controllable way   or if the
semblance of verisimilitude   had once come out of a human mouth
or was just   a performance piece encoded   with the software
finding out its voice

it had been fun   but less and   less   and   command prompts
didn't fit in with the way we thrashed   and trashed   the punch-
pocked   plasterboard   schoolrooms always practising

the episode   replayed this too   in the monotone
unerring evenness of delivery   bypassing the studio effects
the equalisation   stuck in mind to leave just   the hook
of the poem   finding its pulse   with anyone free to listen

PERMANENT
Cat Turhan

a comedian on the radio said
       their mouths were ovals of despair

hurricane-namers on the BBC
       said after the earthquake it was
                     worse

the world behind its thick skin
answered

I take a pulse

       you know when you need a really good cry

you strap yourself
       to a rock

Pyrrha knows what I mean
       when I say they never call storms

something sexy like Aslan or Sheba —

       I want to be washed in permanent blue

Bernadette offers saturation
       streets with weak tea
that smell
       letting the body know danger
in the hospital dede finds
       the only Turkish speaking nurse says

if he can't go home he will   defenestrate

the vocabulary of anger multiplies at the rate of
                                                    bacteria

dad speaks five languages translates blame
                                     into every one

PROTEUS IN MOURNING
Dominic Leonard

explicitly the sea,
dun. the wide sea and sudden.
depth. excess. come on.
he and his hair-breadth.
he and herons swooping
by, bodily.
he peers down, down
to feel his insides, he
can feel them being in there.
he sees the miles themselves
like chains under the water,
where he goes – out of sound,
the tune of his hearing
channelled into the dark back
nowhere, no time. come on.
a buckle in the sea.
a leaning on the shove
of the sea, sealnosing
up the cold rocks and rugged.
he takes flesh from his trough.
he stretches it on his bones.
he takes form from the sea
and hangs it on his bones.
form, what a mouthful.
come on. come on.
he can feel the trout's
furious icepack engines
rattling like gunboats.

he can feel the air
starting there and pouring
all the way down to here.
a boat passes over
and he feels the deepdown
cello hum of it,
beneath sound, where he stays.
he wraps the shape.
of his shape. around
his shape. the margins
of an anguish

ISSUE SEVEN

September 2023
Edited by Pascale Petit

PASCALE PETIT was born in Paris and lives in Cornwall. She is of French, Welsh, and Indian heritage. Her eighth collection of poetry, *Tiger Girl* (Bloodaxe, 2020), was shortlisted for the Forward Prize and for Wales Book of the Year. Her seventh, *Mama Amazonica* (Bloodaxe, 2017) won the inaugural Laurel Prize, the Royal Society of Literature Ondaatje Prize, and was a Poetry Book Society Choice. Four previous collections were shortlisted for the T.S. Eliot Prize. Her debut novel, *My Hummingbird Father*, is forthcoming from Salt Publishing in 2024.

METEMPSYCHOSIS
Alana Chase

I peel back the envelope flap like a Hershey's Bar.
The letter's from the scientist, informing me
he's been told to put down the white-tailed doe,
scotch the panther, their spots just beginning
to fade. He says no one's certain how it can be,
but the two specimens are really the same animal.
He's being kind. We both know he means me.
There are only so many ways you can beautify
the truth. Inside me are a pair of zoic hearts
pulling blood from a single pool. This maiden year,
I was meant to have made them morph, but I couldn't
bring them to a shared field of grass without one
making a meal of the other. So I let my homebody
beasts know no bounds. And when they fought,
I watched the bloodshed like a slasher film,
or a documentary on tax fraud. I think of
what I might become when the scientist is done
and I'm brought back better. Maybe it's the gulls
swirling the air above me, this letter held tight
against the faunal theater roaring in my chest,
but I feel I'd quite like to turn into something
small and volant and sure, with a mouth
that only opens to scream or to sing.

POSTPARTUM

Erica Hesketh

In another world, I'm sure I laced my tea with fenugreek.
Yes, I dressed my front door with garlands of straw and pine
and lay in state for five days, while a young woman
from the village rubbed salt into my swollen feet.
In another world, I know I rested for the full thirty days.
I avoided hot baths. Or I avoided cold baths. My hair lay
tangled on the pillow like a serpent's shed skin. I saw it.
In another world, I shied away from men, shielded them
from my unholy body, the uncertainty slipping
like scarlet silverfish down my thighs. My sheets were
buried quickly under the floorboards. In another world,
the colostrum dried out in my breasts. Or I nursed freely,
day and night, day and night, never offending any ghosts.
In another world, I packed my bags and returned
to my mother's house, to be fed, washed, taught what
a mother was, at last, to be grateful. In another world,
I must have been surrounded for a hundred nights by wild,
wise, luminous women who stroked my cheeks and wept
for the beautiful things I had lost. In another world,
I may have slept for forty days while those exact women
mixed elixirs from angelica root, honey, cracked seaweed,
their heavy plaits thudding like boots on their backs.
The questions drying out in my mouth. What is. Why did. Would it
have. In another world, other hands may have soothed my baby
while I watched from under a thick blanket. Maybe I ate
nothing but hot foods to counteract my feminine nature,
so spongy and unfinished. In another world, they may have
hoisted me above an open fire and left me to sweat it out.
To cure. To counteract. We have no way of knowing.

AUBURN
Millie Guille

August failed early with bathers in its mouth
which means either: I never really loved you,
or either: I never loved myself.

And the leaves will fall, or they won't
and the bathers drown, or don't
and the sun will spread her hips in the sky
for shorter   and shorter   periods

with no-one to hold her at night.
I said no-one to hold her at night.

And God won't return my calls
no-one catches the light as it falls
when I try, it scorches my hands

leaves blood where it lands.

NOT ABOUT URBAN EXPLORERS
Stuart Charlesworth

There's a pack of students
      tearing around
the gutted aquarium halls
of the old telephone exchange,
the condemned terrace row,
the manor house, the office block,
      burgled bare,
shorn of cables and lead-lined roofs.

The rough-looking kids
from the local school
filming their adventures
down the sewers,
      they post their tour
of the ward I worked on
before it closed down. Their commentary
on what they think happened
in the ghostly 'Asylum',
their Scooby-Doo theme park,
is unrecognisable to me.

Disturb that wet, decaying pile
of leaves in your back yard.
Lift the manhole cover
leading down
to blue-green moss
      and mould, steadily
eating the sofa you never bought

with the lover you only picked up in a club
and had an awkward one night stand with.

The sofa hangs precariously
        on and off a joist
in a gaping hole in the sinking floor;
and there in the corner is a cake,
a rotting time capsule
of mushrooms and spores
with a miniature you
and that lover on top.

Eighteen and freshly free
from home, I joined any university club
that would have me. Signed up
to the caving soc. for weekends away
        in borrowed Land Rovers,
electric lamps mounted

on mud-scuffed helmets,
wetsuits under boiler suits.
Changing by the roadside

in the Mendips at dawn,
then tracing the thin river
        into darkness
then darker than that.
Past delicate stalagmites,
tiny blind spiders.
        Till the river cuts
through the limestone seam,
sculpting a cliff face
beneath the hillside.

Not enough for some —
there was a splinter group
who never stopped talking
      about disused mines.
How they wanted to descend
from wrecked pump-houses.
How they wanted to read
the names of the miners
that were on the last shift
before closure,
      carved into
the hard-packed earth.

Well I have mining blood
      or so I believe
in my maternal line,
but I would not go
into those manmade underworlds,
no not for love nor money.

Even walking in daylight,
      sunburnt September, around
the ancient industrial ruins
of the Ding Dong mine in Cornwall,
I looked on the stones
in the still-standing walls
with suspicion.
As if some had been lifted
from the megalithic circles
      near Boskednan
and the surrounding moorlands —

the malevolence in the gorse —
the perfectly circular pit-shaft
was a bottomless challenge
I fought to ignore —

    I think I know
what I would do
down there:

The gallons of water
I'd pour on the ground
    until out of the soup of it
would rise my biological father.
And I'd hold his head
while the earth filled his mouth,
his nostrils and lungs,
and while that subterranean
    quickpool
hardened again into concrete.

Then, perhaps while quietly singing
a throwaway tune to myself
and without ever
    looking back,
I'd climb out.

DREAMBABY
Chloe Elliott

I am in a volcano
that is lava without red which
is mean of my mind but I am at
least awarded Sophie who I cling
to on a dragon pool-float as
our bald crowns sparkle over
the sulphuric gas before
she is rushed away to brunch
with her children and I am reminded
of my barrenness with a tethered
kind of calm where I am forced under
rock as I search for my dead children
by their feet but there are no toes
only things that resemble frozen crabsticks
or trick birthday candles where everyone
is too white to be mine
so I go back & follow the loss
all the way home to the first water bear
to exist and here I find myself suckered
into a crater that functions
the way any room does with gravity
like one of those primordial waiting rooms
that run by normal force & petrol sponges
& midwives that suck on the carpel
of lilies as they stack the blue roll
like flames in a bin today this woman
told me about her waterbirth she smiled
she stroked my cheek said the whole thing
was easy like shooting out a bullet

PRIN / CESS / PARK / MAN / OR

Gemma Barnett

I – <u>cess</u>

i'm listening to a podcast that recognises
everything as a construct. in that case i
don't know the origin of anything. a chain
dropped into descending water proves all
is traceable if you haul yourself toward it.
maybe it's a long time ago when the jails
picked illness like a scabby knee when
asylums came to take out the poor, beat
them into submission like his front door
last week, boot driving through the letter-
box. i wasn't there but i hear wailing
was thrown in a cell. i know bars cast
stripes down wet faces, his eyes now
holes made by extinguished cigarettes,
remembering his brother's body left in
their house turned over.

i mean to say: on Wednesday when they
finally let him home, now alone, brother's
blood the carpet crust, the police stuck
planks of wood across their own damage
saying

that'll do
with the scum they let in
anyway

                      on Thursday when we drove up to help
                      clean splintered needles, he asked me
                      for a tenner. i clutched my pocket searching
for the origin of punitive.

II – <u>Prin</u>

my 13th birthday party was a dewy sleepover.
the glamourised teen movie fun turned horror when a thin girl's
mother asks if she's taking her medication – refusal

ends in multiple murders of good un-pilled girls. a shower
curtain dragged underground. my fingers radicalised
the beanie baby. Four hours away, a boy –

almost known as Harry Styles, is tucked in bed   white
bread cling-filmed. he sleeps soundly. i find the surreptitious
floor of my parents' room; can't undress the movie from my flesh.

III – <u>Park</u>

we were driving
to Grovelands
when the car crashed –

i learnt to wear
a seatbelt
head nodding free.

IV – <u>or</u>

                    or
              could it be
         that inside that car
      the clock was the wrong
       year inside the wrong
year my family sits round
     a tired table trying
       to chew so silence
       doesn't get angry –
         holding hands
           in-between
           knives and
             forks

V – <u>Man</u>

One Direction, Busted, The Wanted, JLS have all lived in Princess Park Manor, a luxury complex in Barnet once a mental hospital home to 2,500 patients. After years of complaints on January 27, 1903 one of the wards caught fire. 52 women were killed, many of them trapped in their beds.

what i mean to say by all this
is i don't know how to say
any of this but by recurring
dissociative dream as far
back as memory hauls me.
they sit at the edge of my
little bed, an impending choir
of sprechstimme saying:

deep breathing activates the other
nervous system. we found stillness
in Tottenham Cemetery. don't pass
us your microphone Harry –

the PA system in the corner
is temperamental. last week it edged
so close – can't hear ourselves think.
have you lot noticed

your yawns don't work? even
in bed you don't get what you need.
go on, crawl up our legs, suffocate
at the waistline. things used to be

safe near a stomach – bless them.
we've been waiting and so what:
you bought 52 deck chairs? that won't
solve a thing now our bodies are smoke.

Epilogue – <u>cess</u> (part II)

what i mean to say is
i don't know what to say
on Friday when there's
nobody left to attend
his funeral

SIMULATION

Eira Elisabeth Murphy

The probability that I am not real
gets greater the longer I live.
Before bed, I imagine dissolving
into numbers, translating my thoughts back into fractions.
I imagine this process of simplification
to be like unwinding wool.
A bathroom that must once have existed is supplanted by the white tiled dome
I wish up in replacement.
I make this the site of my brother's almost choking,
a hot rash of fists and hands forced down throats.
I remember that pain lives in the body,
not in the contortions of air around
what I can no longer say,
the slow morse code blink
of a computer cursor.
A flight of magpies is a glitch on the evening, puckering air and blue light.
I reach for you blindly.
This ritual feels like throwing stones.
I wait for the resolution of broken water.
I say *tonight the earth is round like any other planet*
and I feel my liver unmoor itself, float upwards
and out towards you.
I describe a view from my window
in old colours
and the initials of lost people.
In my imagined bathroom, I do not notice that
I am already in mourning for you.

I imagine the shape of your last smile,
do not stop to think about what I must later convince myself is true.
I lose control of my breathing,
safeguard memory
in cold water.
I dream that I have destroyed my voice
and all its terrible brokenness sits round me.
I dream I am a computer screen going dark
then flashing up a constellation,
white-hot peep holes, hair-line fractures,
or fish swimming flat against purple,
each scale blurring into
tiny pixellated squares of coded bone.

FATHERS WHO WERE SOLDIERS CAN'T PLAY HIDE AND SEEK, IT'S IN THE MANIFESTO SIS

Yaz Nin

There was a god here once
my father told us in his mother's empty house

My sister then six
leaning against a white wall overcrowded with family portraits
moaned with braided hair and pink flip flops

But why can't we play hide and seek?

My sister now 27
still hasn't forgiven our father
she makes a show and tell
when playing hide and seek with her children

See Baba this is how it's done!

I did not tell her
last summer
when rearranging the portraits in the godless house
I forced her children to wriggle their fingers in the bullet holes
gold framed portraits had been hiding

IN THE ROCKPOOL
Kristian Evans

Midnight syllables on the black
water of the rock pool, whisper
of salt retreating into crystal
mind of limpet and gutweed,
untranslatable speech. I recognise
nothing in this mirror. Broken
shells and bones, a cloud of ink
remembering itself, articulating
a psalm of mineral health. When
all this is over I will run away.
I will run and I won't look back.
Bladderwrack and barnacle Kabbalah,
digital sweat, micro-plastic alphabet.

SEVEN OTHER THINGS GEORGE FLOYD IS DOING RIGHT NOW

Thembe Mvula

when walking his daughter to school, a colony of blood
coloured ants halts them in their tracks.
they watch tiny bodies zip through a cracked
pavement like a miniature underground railroad.
george recounts the african proverb: *an ant on its feet can
do more than an elephant on its back.* a police van

drives past them, keeps going.

after inventing a sustainable solution to aviation travel,
george lives off the grid; grows his own produce
and tells the best fireside stories.
in the life where he followed his childhood dream
of becoming a professional basketball player,

he's a workaholic, knows the indentations of
a spalding sphere on his fingertips better than
the softness of his wife's brown skin,
everyone is thrilled that he is living
to his fullest potential.

george has obama as a guest on his late night show – *floyd's weekly roundup.*
he interviews him on his latest cook book. they discuss legacies
of black billionaires and round off the show with
a live rendition of midnight train to georgia.

he's a ballet dancer

after a standing ovation for his haunting performance
at the lincoln centre, he huddles under a hoodie
on his way back home.

he's the poet laureate of the united states.
his face fixed on dime coins,
a national treasure.

he's with his mother in jamaica.
when he calls out to her, she responds,
holds his hand and smiles, he is seven years old again,
fear still unfamiliar to the vocabulary
of his breath.

ISSUE EIGHT

November 2023
Edited by Harry Josephine Giles

HARRY JOSEPHINE GILES is a writer and performer from Orkney, living in Leith. Their verse novel *Deep Wheel Orcadia* was published by Picador in October 2021 and won the 2022 Arthur C. Clarke Award for science fiction book of the year. Their poetry collections *The Games* (Out-Spoken Press, 2018) and *Tonguit* (Freight Books 2015) were between them shortlisted for the Forward Prize for Best First Collection, the Saltire Prize and the Edwin Morgan Poetry Award. They have a PhD in Creative Writing from the University of Stirling. Their show *Drone* debuted in the Made in Scotland Showcase at the 2019 Edinburgh Fringe and toured internationally, and their performance What We Owe was picked by the Guardian's best-of-the-Fringe 2013 roundup – in the "But Is It Art?" category.

THE IRISH QUESTION
Fin Keegan

After Manchán Magan

To pick up a *cloch* and think it a *cloch* or
To pick up a *cloch* and think it a *stone* or
To pick up a *stone* and think it a *cloch* or
To pick up a *stone* and think it a *stone*.

HELL IS A DUMP INTO THE PYMMES BROOK
Francis-Xavier Mukiibi

My black is found   trenched at the base of the Lea
    missing-poster-bodies   distorted voices beneath which I am
        coarse fuzz of algae coating   the surface quiet

    missing-poster-bodies   distorted voices beneath   I am
        coarse fuzz of algae coating the surface   quiet
            breathless   succumbing to a mould of purgatory

        coarse fuzz of afro coats the surface   quiet
            breathless   succumbing to a mould of ~~purgatory~~ purge
    eyes   curdled-milk-yellow   search for God in the fore

            breathless   succumbing to mould   purged
    eyes   curdled-milk-yellow   search for God   in the fore
sunken bicycles   wheelless   converted into crucifixes

    eyes curdle   milk-yellow   search for a God   in the fore
sunken bicycles   wheelless   convert into crucifixes
        their faint blinking lights the edge of flushed flesh

sunken bicycles   will-less   convert into crucifixes
        their faint blinking lights the edge of flushed flesh
    its birthmark   familiar   is this how out-of-body feels   how I bear

        faint blinking lights   the edge of flushed flesh
this birthmark   familiar   is this how out-of-body feels   how I bear
        witness to my body's twists   how it takes shape in wreckage
    this birth   familiar   is this how out-of-body feels   how I bear

         witness to my body's twists   how it takes shape in wreckage
if I die here in the marshes   the melanated man will hunch up

         witness my body's twists   how it takes shape in wreckage
if I die here in the marshes   de-melanated man will hunch up
         my limbs   my body becoming traffic-cone-bright

if I die here in the marshes   de-melanated man will hunch up
                  my limbs   my body becoming traffic cone   bright
    against tarmac noir   as if to say   *turn   lest you wish to become this*

                  my limbs   my body   become traffic cone   bright
    against tarmac noir   as if to say   *turn   lest you wish to become this*
will I be publicly rested   surrounding towers

    against tarmac noir   as if to say   *turn   lest you wish   to become this*
will I be publicly rested   the surrounding towers
         a brick stove from which I burn   an impromptu cremation

STRATHCLYDE PENSION FUND
Silas Curtis

I: strathclyde pension fund

close to 500 quid wages in a padded envelope
not tinkered by bankers who will cave-in yemin.

      i practice my continental affect in
      the high-yield region.

            the microwave
                sky.

                      the rich r not human
                      or they r the only humans idk.

the kelvin is clean
because i am smart and stuff

my body feels nature
not bureaucracy-hale.

II: gated commune

the scarcity
mountain the

hung garden of
derivatives

all guns pointed
@ deckchair

i have peace
in my old age

u have life-

expectancy
statistics.

who do u sell
2 when u r

the devil
already.

III: no one lives vicariously

withered
by bourgeois
sun tunnel

crisis at the heart of
id. w/ career trajectory

swaths who can
blow 40 – 50
on drink in one sitting

+ failure to accumulate
   in linear manner.

i ride my bike

& withdraw from luxury of peaceful
feeling

i ride it around govan's
thales optronics. the

uneven distribution of
stillness /
occupation.

IV: & now i move thru the boss' time.

imperial
flyover
trails powdered
loop-de's.

the
grayscale
dispenses my wages.

DAUGHTER, IN RELATION TO

Betty Doyle

one or both her parents. *See also:* Father. *See also:* 'Somebody's daughter'. In relation to protection, possession. Antonym: worthy. *See also:* Mother. Synonym: responsible. Synonym: synonymous.

also *verb* meaning to shoulder
also *verb* meaning to become perfect without status, to become mother without baby or age, to listen without response as in *She daughtered the youngest son* or *She daughtered the divorce* or *She daughtered the dirty floors and daughtered greasy plates and daughtered the garden, the sheets, the bins, the milk, and the eggs*
also *adj* meaning buffered
also *narrative* as in *the narrative of the eldest buffer will never get old because the burden is never-ending*
also *statistics* as in *99% of eldest buffer trauma wouldn't exist if _____ just _____*
See *also*: SI unit Pascal
also *noun* meaning buffer as in *We wanted a son but we got a buffer* or *We have a buffer and a son* or *My buffer is my best friend* or *Eldest buffer's brain compartments be like: mother trauma father trauma sibling trauma* or *are you the eldest buffer and hold every sort of responsibility and burden, take all the heat and get all the fresh trauma* or *are you normal* or *you either break the generational curse of eldest buffer trauma or die trying* or *Just wait until you have a buffer of your own* or *I can't believe my buffer will never have a buffer of her own*
also *noun* – meaning not found

NOTE ON PASSING
Leyla Çolpan

But you knew it would be like this—one moment the neoplasm looks almost like an infant, then the wet sound of maternal instinct shifting open as you coax him, brush and plait his snotty off-pink lump of cells   *There there*   making the biopsy out like the avuncular cheek-pinch that it isn't   *It won't hurt*   *I love you Please don't kill me*   proffering the good-boy lollipop as if to say   *I'm sorry*   *I would like to live*   as question first, before (is it a question still)   *I want to live!*   The stupid baby grin of the body rejoining: Prove it   Well wasn't it you Back then   Was you   Who imagined   The kid brother skipping beside you down your almost-girlhood's lonely silly tunnel; then it was your mother: her skin that leapt and multiplied, blackening as if   to meet your want. Now stutter is his native tongue   Is yours   Like this   Simile   Pitter-patter   *Ba-ba*   *An-na*   His cells repeat themselves, his cells rename you. His voice pleats inside the body-cavity like a spoiled organ, knotting what you'd like   with what it isn't. What else could such a sound have coaxed from you—this teary mitotic thing that looks back up at you as if   about to call you *mother*—when your want alone had used to be enough. When you hadn't even had to ask.

AMIANTHUS INCEPTION OF DYSFUNCTION
Cogwheel

What reticent stab rebellions
these crazy cats can have.
        Attendant of tiny acts
            that here are proven vast.
On reinforced short crust tiles
under a crippling vibrissae mass
of fletched lichen missile fire.
All falls to slowing amber's sterile slag —
a serous sample. Eyelids forced-wide,
jar-trapped.

The opposite of living is
to be made to watch life.
        Such small deviation
           from designated tasks.
For all time cilia little angel hairs will pluck
particles of petty crime that cling from scratch,
poised as terminal flags. Nine lives will suck
out eternal tunes as air goes past
with each choked breath that lasts
and lasts, and lasts.

BIG UTOPIA
Caroline Wiygul

I imagine a daughter—a child can be anything, I'm aware, but she feels a mirror
of me & so:
a daughter— and you, genderless love. For us, inosculation, a marriage of trees &
for her a christening into a veneration of river ecologies, no talk in this dream
of mass extinction, no talk of desertification my daughter alights to school
against a sky painted in gentle film grain. So I have this tiny utopia, this
20-minute city, & I have the version where everyone is a blank
where everyone used to be, shadowless shadows—& I know
somewhere there's a bigger dream to be had, brash &
serious & anarchist & engineered with clay we can
rewet & rewet, but here, in the shrink, it's always:
just one old forest left, just an emerald ash not
hollowed by bores, just moss, just a worn-out
couch, just a curry dinner, a copper pot, just
a window that it is safe to open, just not
the prophesied blast of methane, just
to touch the top of your hand with
my fingertip, just a pen & paper,
just the same four things to do
each morning, just a life
my child might
forgive
me

f-

o-

r

.

My

frie-

nds

& I are

accused

of the sin of

expectation: I don't

think the world owes me

but don't I owe the world

a gentle life, a part of myself,

a dedication or some new religion

based on these whittled wants: past these,

above them, in what they require, I can almost

imagine—

WITH
Alia Zapparova

voices

      walked   way way way

                                                                                            We

                                                                                           We

                                                                                           We

                                                                                           We

                                                                                           We

                                                                                           We

weak wet what when

                    whispering   world world   you you you you

SOUNDING SOIL

Agata Maslowska

Sounding Soil of a Forest

Vwwvwvw wuwuwuwuzzzzm mzzzmzzzmzzz zzzzzzzzuwww mlmlmluwmluwmluw zzzsssszzzssszzz shshshshshshsh zhzhzhz msssmssmssssmmmm mmmmssssss vtrrrrrr vtreeeeee mmzzzzz sooosssssooosoooosooo ffffzzzfzzzfzzzzzz nnnnaaannnaaanna

Sounding Soil of the Seabed

Wawawawawawawa wowowwowo wuwuwuuwuw owowowow uwuwuwuwuw awawawawa wooowwooooowwww wuuwwuush shshhhshhh sh ssshhuuwwwww shuuwwwwwshhhh owowowsh eawoeawoea eaeaeaeaeaw weaweaweaweashhhh weashh ishhhhh

Sounding Soil of a Meadow

Grrgrrgrr grrrr tkrrrtkkkkrrr tk tkkkkkk sheeeshe grr grrrrgrrrrr shuushuuu vzzzzz vzzzzzz vzzzzzz bruuuummmzzzzzz brumzz katikitikitikitiki grrrrgrrrrruummmzzzhhhh vuuuvuuuuu wushhh thrtkrthruuuuuu gzzzzgzzzzbvgzzzzhhh vzevrtrrrrtrrrt tktktkkk

Sounding Soil of a Nuclear Plant

Glglglglglglgl ungrungrungr rarararara dedededede glglglglglglgl ungrungrung: rarararara dedededede glglglglglglgl ungrungrungr rarararara dedededede glglglglglglgl ungrungrungr rarararara dedededede glglglglglglgl ungrungrungr rarararara dedededede

Sounding Soil of a Potato Field

- -
- -
- -
- -

ST. FRANCIS

Shani Cadwallender

Spring's eternal fox-piss park
in ivy's chokehold blossoms
spectacular blotting asphalt white
like dog-chewed bread-husks indigestible
mulching notice do not feed the pigeons it encourages vermin squirrel
eyes dough hungrily and I
under standing scale-sky try
to weigh what's owed
how to repay
with interest
with investment
bubble- joy of you unfurled
the hope of happening
upon you
windblown

ISSUE NINE

January 2024
Edited by Fran Lock

FRAN LOCK is a some-time itinerant dog whisperer, the author of numerous chapbooks and thirteen poetry collections, most recently *Hyena!* (Poetry Bus Press, 2023), shortlisted for the T.S. Eliot Prize 2023, and *'a disgusting lie': further adventures through the neoliberal hell-mouth* (Pamenar Press, 2023). *White/Other* (The 87 Press, 2022), a collection of hybrid lyric riff, was a Poetry Book Society Recommendation. Fran was the Judith E. Wilson Poetry Fellow at Cambridge University (2022-23), researching feral subjectivity through the lens of the medieval bestiary. Fran's other work includes the chapbook *Forever Alive* (Dare-Gale Press, 2022), and the critically acclaimed work of 'queer mourning' *Hyena! Jackal! Dog!* (Pamenar Press, 2021).

Fran is Commissioning Editor at the radical arts and culture cooperative Culture Matters, where she most recently edited the mammoth anthology *The Cry of the Poor* (2021). She is a member of the new Editorial Advisory Board for the *Journal of British and Irish Innovative Poetry*, and she edits the Soul Food column for *Communist Review*. Fran teaches online for Poetry School, and she is the co-host of the cross-cultural poetry podcast Social yet Distanced with her cousin Jack Varnell. Fran is a super proud pit bull parent. She lives in Kent.

THE FIRST 7 DAYS AS A WITCH

Natalie Moores

Day 1: Turn you into a witch so we can do this fresh new life together

Day 2: Beam green at the mountaintop

Day 3: Work up courage to remove a newt's eye (me) and a frog's toe (you)

Day 4: Cry almost all day about the newt (me) and the frog (both)

Day 4 (much later): Eat a child, whole

Day 5: Put that man's name in a deep chest so no one can hear his shrieking

Day 6: Bristle at the ghouls at the base of our necks. Some witch business feels familiar

Day 7: Hold tight to who we were and who we are. Soar.

A WORMHOLE IS

Debmalya Bandyopadhyay

An imaginary tunnel through space and time, as Papa had explained to me seven springs after my birth. I was disappointed that it wasn't a home for worms. How I wished it was a room cocooned in mud, where the Papa worm comes back home early evening and smokes a cigarette by the window. Next to him, Mama worm knits a scarf with the last of daylight. Between them, just a lost gaze reflecting the bedroom bulb's insincere mellow.

Since then, I've folded myself in crevices. Like an animal inching through the heart's charcoal tunnels, a refugee dreaming of another home. My rooms are now filled with the damp songs of absence, each note an elegy to the past. All I've learnt of the worm is that no matter how bright the world outside, it crawls into a hypnotic dark: the body's lyric hooked to that magnetic tune, offering itself as a lantern.

A QUESTIONNAIRE FOR THE FURIES

Katherine Collins

1. When women
   - a. call out for the dread, is it you who answers?
   - b. rage fruitlessly, is it you who bear it?

2. What may we infer from the fact that your awfulness begins
   - a. with the sound of awe?
   - b. and ends in repletion?

3. Do you customarily torment men because they made you as the personification of their deepest shame
   - a. and is that why you are exquisite?

4. Why did you steal torches from a funeral?
   - now we reach the essence of the poet's current preoccupation

5. Was it a punishment to the deceased? What had they done? Was it something to warrant
   - a. extinguishing the lights
   - b. [at] their funeral?

6. And finally, like torches, does rage burn out or up?

SELF-PORTRAIT AS MY GHOST, WHO WILL EVENTUALLY HAUNT YOU

Rachel Bruce

I am a half-formed notion,
a pin you think you've stepped on but cannot find,
a wanton breeze tending to your cheek.
You have forgotten me even as you walk into the room
you came to find me in.
I see the way you scratch your nose when you are alone.
I sit in the back of the cupboard, reading ingredient lists
and crying into vitamins.
I backpack between rooms
threaded to your shadow by a strand of your hair.
Mine is still red — death does not revert you to factory settings.
I am a hermit crab refusing to change its shell.
I am the empty film in your camera,
the defunct intention to capture a moment.
I cannot touch my fingers to your hand,
instead I tug pathetically at your bedcovers,
paw at the lights to make them flicker.
I do not know what you believe.
I wish I knew how you thought of me,
your smile a spiral shell upon my back.
Sometimes there is a light. It comes from the fridge
but is darker, cooler.
I have to hide away on those days,
must not let it find me curled inside your jumpers.
Haunting is like burning eggs and having to eat them.
But better to be this non-thing
than to have you vanish from me,

to have lost you in the way
I always feared I would.

ST NICHOLAS REFUSES HIS MOTHER'S MILK ON FASTING DAYS

Aysar Ghassan

A boy in a tiny gingham collar, caramel gelled furrows parting his straw-coloured hair, gives me the finger through the bottom half of the front passenger window of his mother's smart German saloon.

Boys, dots on playing fields, too close to the woods, running from older boys with more developed quadriceps, hoping to make it home before getting their heads kicked in. Each, the apple of mother's eye, a gemstone pocketed on the exodus from Eden, kissed on both cheeks by aunts jostling for position.

CORRIGENDUM

JP Seabright

After Anthony (Vahni) Capildeo

For: *everything is fine*, read: *everything is fire*
For: *hatreds*, read: *hat trends*
For: *coup d'état*, see also: *cup of tea*
Ditto: *panellists = penalties*
For: *angels*, read: *bagels*
For: *family*, read: *famine*
For: *accelerate*, see also: *ancestor*
For: *contested*, read: *consented*
For: *visitor*, see: *visor*
For: *unite*, read: *smite*
Ditto: *picketing = ticketing*
For: *our rooms are not equipped with irons*,
Read: *our rooms are not equipped with icons*
For: *mosquitos*, see also: *inquisitor*
For: *the power of the ballot*, read: *the power of the hello*
For: *images*, see also: *things*
For: *read the signs*, read: *read the sighs*

THE BEATIFICATION OF CATHERINE OF SIENA
Sam Furlong

Unlike the plague-boys who whipped themselves to
salvation outside the churches, Catherine of Siena
knew the value of private pain. She cruised to sleep
with a sharpened pike for clandestine castigation.
Here is my body, she told Him, *may it be an anvil
for Thy beatings.* In her final days, only the Eucharist
passed her lips; happy to live and die on his flesh alone.
When there is too much desire and not enough God,
we must turn something inward— a pike or an appetite.
(I always wait for my dates to use the bathroom before I swallow
The last of my dinner.) Still, Catherine learned early
they would never make her a priest or a prophet
but if she died well enough, she would be granted a word
that looks both like beautiful and beating.

YOU COME THROUGH THE SOIL

Jon Alex Miller

*After 'You come through the needle' by Gagan Gill,
translated by Kushal Khandhar.*

you come through the soil and I through the trowel
love   sometimes I through the soil and you
through the trowel   what work is this we do
love   together through the centuries
what digging is this   that does not finish
we throw around our sweat and laugh   waiting
for galaxies to fall through our shovels
        onto the dirty sheets of our messy bed
the days have gone   love   all the years too
no end in sight   love   this bed has no edges
sometimes the soil
        sometimes the trowel
what garden of stars turns   turns with our toil

THE MEN IN COMPANY VANS WHO GIVE LIFTS TO AWAY MATCHES

Patrick O'Donoghue

Of Sons and Co. and Ltd.
The slide door, the bandy gait – the inheritance.
Hauling nothing but hauntology,
and the leaden babel
of too many kids to pretend to love equally.

Toughened glass panels
reinforcing the bone zone behind driver's seat
factotums safe and serene
in a shatterproof surround.

But now even the road studs turn red
as those marmalising matchday manias.
Figments of a flag-flying halcyon flicker
like target fixation on an infinite bend.

Nails and screws rust
and rattle for their steel deliverance.

Beyond the clubhouse cloister,
the birthday bottle bores
and DIY dignity,
awaits a structure fallen to bits.

What strange birds have since
nested in the old treehouse
that came long before the van
and all it took to be a man?

QUEER CLIMATE

Julia Ireland

I run hot in a cold country,
heard a butch poet today,
ran hotter. Her hairline's
a protest, she fights my fight
and even I flinch at her use of line
breaks. A statement in every
full stop, the world fears her
jawline. She could take this town,
this country, your body.
What's being queer got to do with climate change?
Ask a Roman when their empire
fell off the earth. Ask her across the street
who tosses the word gay
like a can out a car window.
Bold print says World on Fire. I say
the Ice Age is creeping near
and the warmth of our neighbours

dropping a degree each year.

ISSUE TEN

March 2024
Edited by Inua Ellams

INUA ELLAMS: Born in Nigeria, Inua Ellams is a poet, playwright & performer, graphic artist & designer and founder of: The Midnight Run (an arts-filled, night-time, urban walking experience.), The Rhythm and Poetry Party (The R.A.P Party) which celebrates poetry & hip hop, and Poetry + Film / Hack (P+F/H) which celebrates Poetry and Film. Identity, Displacement & Destiny are reoccurring themes in his work, where he tries to mix the old with the new: traditional African oral storytelling with contemporary poetics, paint with pixel, texture with vector. His books are published by Flipped Eye, Akashic, Nine Arches, Penned In The Margins, Oberon & Methuen.

ODE TO PIERRE

Iain Bleakley

I smoked a puff of Pierre's joint on top of the Unité D'habitation. I don't really smoke but I wanted to say I had a joint on the rooftop of Corbusier, looking out over the sea and the mountains, down at the crow that kept flying and landing photogenically on that iconic concrete staircase; *crowbusier*. Pierre's friend curated an art exhibition here and the collective all got high and scribbled on scraps of paper and said 'bleed the rich' and sold them for 400 Euros a pop and Pierre confronted them and said 'zis is not cool zis is not what art iz for' and told them they should do it proper not like that bullshit. From Corbusier we got in Pierre's car stocked up on baguettes and cheese and octopus from the big supermarché where the checkouts were so slow we thought we would never leave. We got to Les Calanques via a treacherous road in this little Toyota which made a *calonk* noise every time we went over a bump. We got out of the car whenever there was a speed bump and decided Pierre should put more air in the tyres. Pierre is Parisian but you'd never know it in the way he scurries around the cliffs. And he's gay though you'd never figure that out either unless he told you or you said something homophobic in his presence. In which case, according to his stories, there are a range of outcomes from a warning to a slap to getting hit by a rock in the back of your skull. But that was Paris Pierre, this is Marseille Pierre where he visits Corbusier in the mornings and dives into the med in his red speedos after lunch using a special diving technique he learned where he punches the water as he hits it to go deeper. During lockdown he'd swim like an eel and dance on the edge of this cliff where the rocks flatten out. Young wild boar would come there looking for a drink and he'd share his water with them.

EASTER LEAVE

Megan McKie-Smith

I bend my neck back. Sixty
    percent Afghan whisky
now in my blood, I'm sure
there's a door somewhere
in the sky I can slip through.
    Down here, on earth
in his nan's old deck chairs
    their floral padding and rust
it's tender silence, until
     he says the most beautiful
stars he's ever seen were over
        Helmand Province. This same sky
these same stars, pulled
    over an ant hill
in the desert where beauty
    was never expected. I think of
him all fatigues and testosterone
    wonder if he told another man to look
up or kept them all to himself.
    He closes his eyes
the taught cord of him now slack
    he unfurls from man to boy.
Someone has cowered at the sight of him.

    Under the stars, burning
on a salt night in April, he lifts an earwig
    out of the fire, his shovel

hand and a twig. He places
        its body on a tall blade of grass
and asks me to cut the onions
        for dinner. For a moment, he looks
like a person who could choose
        his own clothes for a change.
The oven clock flashes 12.00, 12.00
        12.00. I beg for its dumb repetition
to live, suspended with this gentle
        man a while longer
before his knots begin to tighten
        all over again.

WHITE BREAD WHITE SWANS
Lou Hill

we're eating white bread in the sun
behind the allotments
by the side of the dirty little pond
birthed by Banbury Reservoir
now the swans come
past the spot where Jenkins tied rocks
round his bail money   threw it in
then hopped the fence
never to be seen again
the swans swim white elegant
past half-empty Lucozade bottles
bobbing with dogends
loose threads of tobacco in bright orange
fizz   gold stitches
this moment amounts to nothing
but we don't hear that yet
our afternoon is warm & free
from shit-talk   pretending
not to be scared all the time
somewhere a newly-elected minister
maps our lives a takeaway
on his lap one eye on the TV   ketchup
down his dry-cleaned white shirt
but this afternoon breeze brings rocksteady
mellow sweet from Ambrose's flat
carries a whisper in its bowel a bad-line
prank call cracked with muffled laughter
…ccrrk..hahamph you….hehecrrksh…will

have to choose shhhshshha between this
moment & a future…crrrkshhhhahahaha!…
on our backs   too gold everything
I turn my head
to see if you heard it too
your eyes are closed smiling you take a toke
pass me the joint
you don't see the sun
rotting in the sky
the white swans are near now

THE STATUE
Henry St Leger

please, do not topple the statue, the statue was not designed for toppling, insurance does not cover damage in case of toppling, please, do not run your hands over the statue, it may rub off the oxidised layer and remind us of how much gold was stolen to build it, please, the statue is embarrassed enough about this already, please, do not graffiti the statue, it cannot read, please, do not attach items of a sexual nature to the statue, the statue cannot derive pleasure from this, the statue only enjoys being a statue, please, do not tip the statue into the water, the statue cannot swim, please, if you would like the statue removed, use the proper channels, online petition, prayer by torchlight, somewhere else, please, throw yourself in the river, and think about what you've done

UNDER
Rafael Mendes

under *preposition* 1. less than: a fortnight to the college fee's deadline, she is underburdgeted. night shift comes to an end with dockworkers queuing for breakfast rolls. they banter in a mélange of Slavic languages and north inner city accent she fails to untangle. she opens the deli's oven, checks the temperature of rashers, sausages, black puddings, and wonders: if a stack of purple notes comes my way, would I return it? 2. receiving or undergoing the action or effect of: she enters a one-million-euro terrace in Blackrock. the owner gives her a tour of the grounds. walking past the external patio facing the ocean, he says *you don't need to clean the hot tub.* she wonders if a hot tub is similar to a whirlpool, like the one in the hotel where her mother first uttered *chemotherapy.* she adjusts earbuds into her ears, sprays citrus-scented all-purpose cleaning into the tilled walls, and scrubs it as Freddie Mercury sings *under pressure we're cracking / can't we give ourselves one more chance* 3. in or into a position below, beneath, or lower than something: the notification lights up her phone as she empties the club's bins located under an emergency exit. *she's gone.* she relives the morning before when the muscles at the sides of her mother's mouth contracted in a grin as she held the student card in front of the camera. she hears the light thud of a goldfinch against a windshield. somewhere.

MAYBE THE SUN

Ian Irwin

is a disc
of unbridled
fury
a surprise
turn
for
the worse
a mirror
reflecting
our vanity
perhaps
this only sun
is an outpost
for spectres
scattered
sarcasm
of a soft age
maybe the sun
will shrug us
off
an irritant
considering a
distant dream
maybe it does
not
consider us
at all
relentless

its frustration
embodied
by a gurning
ball
demanding
worship
consumes
our attention
hung like
a fat
emperor
greedy
&
bored

SELF-PORTRAIT AS A FAILED EXORCISM
Deborah Finding

No one could say how it happened, exactly. The circumstances were perfect. The Sunday night service at the charismatic church had been delivered — executed beautifully in fact — by the qualified-by-experience pastor: film-star confident, slick, sharp, smooth. The groundwork of guilt had been laid upon her. The hands were laid upon her in familiar ways. There was chanting in which God and the devil were invited to listen carefully. The pastor's pitch and tempo began to rise and rise and rise until with a push of his palm on her head, he shouted in climax *OUT! Satan, we cast you OUT!* She fell to the floor, the congregation watching their favourite scene unfold, nodding, murmuring their pleasure approvingly. She woke, flinch-dazed, stumbled to her feet, newly raised from the dead, encountering the world afresh. Blinking, she began, "What." The throng waited for the "happened?" that would enable them to chorus — *A miracle! Praise Jesus!* — and applaud the heroic conquering they had witnessed. But she stood upright, lifted her jaw, squared her shoulders, stared hard at them all — at him — enunciated slowly and clearly, "The. Fuck.", lack of question mark audible to all, strode out into the night, to the rear-view sound of gasping shock and plastic chairs hurriedly moved in the rush to be of aid, to be the first to comfort him. *You did nothing wrong.*

WHEN I WOKE UP THIS MORNING I TRIPPED OVER DAD

Anna Shelton

an improvement, since for weeks I've been unable to sleep
with him under my pillow, elbows jutting at odd angles,
purpling feet sticking straight out the side.
I showered without him, but stumbled over him on the stairs
going to breakfast; he startled me as I stepped outside,
sat with me as I listened to birds in the garden,
interrupted my train of thought in class. At the table he blocked me,
head down on the hard wood, that final unrelenting view.
He choked me on my food at dinnertime.
When I tried to relax and lean back into an armchair
he was there behind me, making me uncomfortable.
Ever-present dad, suddenly peripheral,
my body doesn't want to leave you behind.

BECAUSE IT'S MUD SEASON AT THE GIRLS' FACILITY

Eve Ellis

girls huddle in the drive before lineup
wearing their clag-spattered jumpsuits
workboots caked like small golems

when the first april evening wafts through
they open their windows   shout
across the bogged lawn   shriek at hills

still hairy with bare trees   haw like donkeys
in the mess hall   drop plastic plates
stamp on smeared egg   their braying

shakes the whole vinyl-sided dorm
staff deduct points   assign extra chores
but they open their throats and bellow   oh

to be thisfuckingloud in the overheated schoolhouse
throwing dictionaries   yanking off doorknobs
hurling a desk at the wall   quaking the floorboards

like spring queens dancing the rage of it
until girl after girl is wrestled to the ground
restrained and mudgutteral   staff clipboards are out

tonight's the deep freeze of cement time-out rooms
an icepatch of sorry and quiet   but you
good girl who threw nothing   thought screaming

was beneath you   sit alone in your dorm room
watching the pale planet of yourself in the glass   heaving
the mud from your lungs   the snowmelt and thick of it

TO THE BLACKENED FIELD
Tracey McEvoy

So, you shipped out
in all your brown glory
fresh from the Trini hills.
Chinee mother and Creole father,
roots in the high plains of Africa
and the lowlands of Scotland.
Born of owners and slaves, locked
in the mesh of money and sex.

In you – in me – is the blood
of three continents. I'm told I pass.
As if it's a test. As if it's not
good enough to prize the
blackness in me. Troubling,
to sing from the seat of privilege,
when what's inside still aches
to be free.

I fixate on who came before,
their wretched journeys across
land and sea, the horrors endured
on ships named *Fortitude*
or *Charming Betty*.

Centuries clawing at the rock,
genes pooled, we kept evolving.
Pulses beating with hybrid vigour.
No time to stop, for the future lies

ahead, just over the next hill.
And all the time, the blood
seeped into the earth,
bringing us home.

I'll winter here, then go
heart in hand, to where
the bones are dug deep.
And there I will look
to the blackened field
of burning cane where
one ancestor raised the whip to another,
and listen
as the fire spits sugar.

ISSUE ELEVEN

May 2024
Edited by Ian McMillan

IAN MCMILLAN is a poet and performer from Yorkshire, as well as a playwright, journalist, and all-round poetry whirlwind. As well as writing and performing his own work, for both adults and children, he is a tireless champion of poetry and the spoken arts, and a campaigner for the arts to be for everybody. He has been a poet, broadcaster, commentator and programme maker for over 35 years. His first collection, *The Changing Problem*, was published by Carcanet in 1980, and since then he has published nearly thirty books. He presents *The Verb* every week on BBC R3 and he's a regular on *BBC Breakfast*, *Coast*, *Pick of the Week*, *You & Yours*, *Last Word* and *The Arts Show*. Previously, Ian was resident poet for English National Opera, UK Trade & Investment, Yorkshire TV's Investigative Poet and Humberside Police's Beat Poet. He's been a castaway on *Desert Island Discs* and a subject of *The South Bank Show*. Cats make him sneeze.

CROWN THE MOMENT
Adam Clifford

Once, there was a four by four that careered to a stop
blacking the country lane. The diagonal wailed
'you've lost her! we'll hold you!' so Uncle Mark poured
out the hunky seat in suit and white, pounded over to Dad
and grabbed the pup in his knitwear. That day I was mature
enough to be left, alone by my Mother's open grave,
work out for myself when to leave, catch up with the party.
Wait for me? No one to watch. The beginning of absence.
Cousin Miriam was second to last, distraught red hair,
watching my age, high shoulders making a triangle
of her narrow stand. She preferred slip-ons. At Auntie
Jane's, we stood on the decking under ambiguity, adults
quantifying me as mum-less. I returned their eyeballs.
A sip of Appletiser. The dark night and Doritos.

BELLY BUTTON ODE

Olivia Tuck

o Alice's rabbit hole   cum little horizon   at too many petit fours marked EAT ME
o mysterious opening   to some Blyton-esque secret passage   I've heard
somewhere that you end at the liver   but I don't know if that's bullshit
and I don't want to fall into mulling over   how *liver*   somehow = *cowardice*
   when wherever you lead to   must be so bold   o lovely grotto
o homely dugout   like the ones in Coober Pedy   I almost see you
   as a shelter   from the knifepoint of noon   or as exactly what you are
   the funniest-shaped relic of   the stream   my mother set rushing
   her gorgeous blood   pouring   through the sluice gate
      bright   and brilliant   into me

IT'S GOOD WE KNEW

Oenone Thomas

if we had made love in that room
over the hometown pub,
we would have torn open
the Artex ceiling
and the space time continuum,

we would never have left
the young farmers at their pints,
the bar woman's uneasy joints,
her woodbine-shade
of shifting chignon.

BARBIE GOES TO THE GYNAE

Amy Dugmore

I want all the apparatus in plastic. I want a glitter-filled IV bag wheeled in on a hot pink trolley. I want a hospital gown trimmed with satin bows and a diamond-studded cannula slotted into my vein. Lurex stitches. Powderpuff swabs. Candy-scented anaesthetic to knock me out, send me off to sweet vacuity. But before I can take a drag, in walks Ken, all heart-eyes and cold hands. No small talk. He picks up a tool, shows me its glinting tip. I know I'm supposed to like its sheen, but all I can see is the face trapped in its silver, warped to its shaft.

I know what he wants and I know not to ask. I learned to play patient a long time ago. I know what to do and I do as I'm told, lay back, heels still on, open my thighs. They don't go as wide as Ken wants. He says he's never seen parts this tight. Says I'm tensing. I can only smile and turn my head as he sticks it in me and I don't feel a thing and I look at the pictures pinned on the wall of cut-out body parts, bodies no legs, bodies no heads bodies with livid organs packed in tight and this isn't me, this isn't inside of me. I take a deep breath, try to remember I'm seamless, picture my plastic-perfect sides, concealing nothing.

Only when he's finished it comes – shards of glitter, a whole smashed up mirror ball in reds and pinks, pours out of me onto the floor.

FROM DÉRIVE

Alex Priestley

15

You find yourself on the top floor of a building. The last flight of stairs seemed especially steep, and the landing especially precarious, like a nest of sticks perched on a high branch. You look around – it's not being used for much. Some flattened carboard boxes are leaning against the wall, a trio of water dispenser bottles are sitting on the floor next to them, and discreetly moving over everything the sweet, pink smell of a cleaning agent. There are no lights on, only the daylight pooling onto the linoleum floor, and then penetrating a little into the corridor. The view out is onto a back entrance – some bins, a parked car. Someone has left a window open – the breeze that enters feels protective, as if to say everything will clear up by itself. The sound of passing voices down below rises up the stairwell and makes the shape of the roof. They are elsewhere, and yet they are here participating in the building's tranquil geometry. Perhaps, sometime, you were leaving a building as part of a fire drill, even if it was when you were at school, and as you were leaving you would hear the alarm, but also many other, fainter, alarms going off in distant parts of the building you did not know. Somehow, you find yourself now in those distant parts, although there is no alarm, only the sense of having struggled to imagine this place sometime before as you heard it in the distance, and of having enjoyed the thought of inhabiting such a far-off, incomplete place, looking, as you left the building, to the sky and the treetops for inspiration as you assembled it, suspended in a daydream. How did you get here? Did someone send you? Did you come looking for something? Did you wander, for a moment?

THE DEVIL HAS A PLAN / FOR US
Ewan John

Saliva is a convection current / hot like blood / dragged / bubbled to the surface / burst like pomegranate through teeth / swallowed by pigeons / wings flustered / pink gullet / innards of a blessing / seeds of rosary // I hold you // between my fingers / between my teeth of a bird / sanguine sentimentality // you hold me // with your tongue / to walk down your words is a dream / sleep can't forget / the feathers thrown / across the room your sky / is yellow / and the sun / is deep blue

THE LAST SUPPER

Nige Tassell

A room. A kitchen.
A table. A chair. A pot to piss in.

Stubble burning through cheeks of alcohol.
Six bottles. Arm's reach.
Three days, tops.

It only takes two. The days beat the drink.
The heart surrenders. The lungs too.
Dead in the chair. Slumped, but stuck. Unslipping.
Just bone and skin and silent organs.
Still.

The doorstep milk sours.
The letterbox fills.
The flies gather for the feast.

MIRROR

Eugene O'Hare

mirror; cold plate of dressed meat,
my long form fiction. if it weren't
for the love of a wet shave
i would never set eyes on you
to give an inch to your distortion.

the trick of me; the gimmickry
of reflection. who falls for this
frame of truth? only my bed knows
my body & its name. i lie there
in dark's mouth stretched into
its swallow, hid under the lid
of something kept from you.

my bed is my wife. she'll have
no glass in the room. we celebrate
the deafness of mirrors & mock
what you mock; the religion of movies
& their over-lit make-up rooms.

BIG TED

Karen Green

Big Ted doesn't seem to be breathing—I can't find a pulse. There's a bullet wound on his chest above the right nipple. Maybe it's just chocolate. His eyes are wide open, staring accusingly at the ceiling. I don't know what to do. I don't even know why he's in my house. They probably threw him out of his last place for bad behaviour—stealing and dealing. There's broken glass on the floor, one of my crystal goblets. He's been drinking his favourite tipple, cherry brandy and advocaat. At least he wouldn't have suffered too much. I try some chest compressions. Can't hear a lot, maybe some wheezing but it sounds more like creaking. He must have passed a few hours ago so this could be the beginnings of rigor mortis. I cover his face with a tea towel and go to bed. I'll make a phone call in the morning.

DEATH OF A SWIMMING TEACHER

Christopher Tracy

She would bellow out instructions
that ricocheted over our heads,
smeared the pool walls
with angry incoherence.

Her eyes were a shark's.
Cold as the deep end.
That first, breath-stealing plunge
to retrieve the rubber brick.

'A sudden severe stomach ache'
or 'flu-like symptoms'
were Monday morning lifelines
every one of us would flounder for.

Though I tried to fight it down
(… *a road accident, children.*),
when the head told us my heart
rose like a float in the water.

ISSUE TWELVE

July 2024
Edited by Tishani Doshi

TISHANI DOSHI is an award-winning poet, novelist and dancer whose work centres the body as a vehicle to explore gender, sexuality and power. Her publications include *Girls Are Coming Out of the Woods, Small Days and Nights*, and *A God at the Door*. She is a fellow of the Royal Society of Literature and a Visiting Professor at NYU Abu Dhabi.

MOTHS

Maya Caspari

In the end the moths get everything   even   our   hearts

sitting in the kitchen
    decked with years
                      I saw my parents
                            gently fading into scraps
          small holes

                            I had not seen before

were waving
in their cheeks

      the moths themselves
                          were spilling
                            from the drawers
                            like overflowing

                                      gasps

their tiny eyes all
focused
as they flew
                      I knew they had no
                                need
                                to care for us

        and still, hopeless
I hoped they would.

                But everything   kept trembling
                                                                    out of form
           the table like a wobbling
           hunk of mountain cheese
                                                                    the plates
                                                              like woven fabric

                              chairs pockmarked
           peppered with spots
                                                              TV a square-cut
                                                              drop, a falling hum
           newsreaders
           fast outgrown
                              by their own mouths
                                                        until only some mouths
                                                                       remained
           sometimes just half a
                                   tongue

           even my hands were stitched   with tiny gaps

                                         Later, I dream
           my father
                                                              in the kitchen
                                                                    once again
           smiling at the stove
           making a soup
           from chicken bones

                                                     like his Prussian grandma

                                                    taught him

sunlight hanging
from his hair

            You look well   I tell him
                                                as if I
                                            cannot see
the clustering moths
 or how his
        edges seem to be softening

                                            beneath
the growing hole   his chin.

That night, I wipe
    the moths off his warm arms
                    ask him
                                    please don't move
                                    too much
                Stay just
                for a while

and the bedroom's half   light seems to bend
                                    at our hands' touch
        under wing shadows
                                gently peeling off
    the edges   the thin frame

LICENCE APPLICATION

Mave Fellowes

My first pet was a human called Denys.
We rescued him from the mammal centre.
He was a smaller than average Caucasian with brown eyes and no beard.
He could sing falsetto and sew his own shifts.
We taught him how to wrestle and tell jokes.
When his stomach began to swell we renamed him Denise.
One morning we came down to the pen to find him panting, his shift soaked.
We called the Medibus to take him away.

I have experience with humans of all ages.
I narrated a documentary about a tribe in the archipelago.
There was one family with four generations.
The great-grandparents had not been culled.
The tribe wore coloured clothes with buttons.
They were hard to track down, the island had no fencing.
Our documentary won a prestigious award.
The island became a destination.

I am a skilled handler of humans.
I can realistically mimic voice and cadence.
I can distract creatively.
I can form diagnoses and administer medicine.
I can operate a collar.
Licence rhymes with science and silence and compliance.
The machine will not tolerate a biter.
Thank you for considering my application.

CHE GUEVARA PLANTS A TREE IN CEYLON
S. Niroshini

Transactions take place in each lover's consciousness

Like when he says *I love you*, he means *I love those parts of you that cut my dark*

The empire used indentured labourers from South India
on its coffee, tea and rubber plantations in the 19th century

[To search for another word for *empire*]

In Kalaripayattu when the leg makes a circular kicking action outwards
it is described as *puram*. When the motion is inwards: *agam*

Agam: the interior landscape, or love poetry, in Tamil from the second century BC

What he said: I want to make love to you again
and again in a thunderstorm

It was a mahogany tree that Guevara planted, once upon a time
in Ceylon

Once upon a time is a lazy translation of the Tamil *ore oru oorile…in that one and only town*

What he said: I want to know language
that bites with its specificity

'*His favourite garden in the world had been the grass garden at Kew, the colours so delicate and various*'

Guevara had been part of a trade delegation from Cuba.
His glamorous interpreter stood next to him in a black and white photograph.

To search for the interpreter's name without success

'Though we have come through / the hot dust of sunbeaten wastelands'
is a line from Ramanujan's translation of the Ainkurunuru

And it was bold of him to think that there was some interiority
or subjectivity that remained

Puram: the public domain, the praise of kings, poets and war

'And there is yet another Cuzco, a vibrant city whose monuments bear witness to the formidable courage of the warriors who conquered the region in the name of Spain...'

Before love, before war, there was—

Screaming is an effective way to reduce the experience of pain

And pain, like all cycles in nature, longs for its completion

---

Notes:

The line beginning with 'His favourite garden in the world...' is from *The English Patient* (1992) by Michael Ondaatje.
The line beginning with 'And there is yet another Cuzco...' is from *The Motorcycle Diaries* (1995) by Ernesto Che Guevara.
'Though we have come through / the hot dust of sunbeaten wastelands' is a line from AK Ramanujan's translation of the Ainkurunuru in *Poems of Love and War* (1985). Ramanujan is believed to be the first to describe agam poetry as the interior landscape

LEAVING THE CITY
Zain Rishi

two brown boys kiss on the ramp by McDonald's
and I have this small feeling just a thought really
that Brum is not this big cultural melting pot it's
more like raw ingredients all sorts of them just
jumbled like the roads at Spaghetti Junction like
ivy scrawled on fancy white-brick pubs like night
falling in Sparkhill and you barely notice because
the air is so thick with sound you can practically
drink it there's this idea that you can take the man
out of Brum but the man is still the boy kissing
another boy goodnight the man is still the ball
bounding along the street at the neighbourhood
cricket match the man still wonders if anything
is ever beautiful beyond nostalgia but honestly
what is the city if not his own anatomy what is
the sky over Ladypool Road peeling from blue
to pink to navy if not another kind of skin what
is the word for the narrow path I will carve onto
this earth is it the rain I'll take to Scotland is it
the rotis I'll keep in the fridge or is it the blood
I felt beneath your lips when we kissed at the
threshold the lamplight bright as a comet the
sheen of rain on your skin when you told me
just go be stupid be beautiful somewhere else

SELF PORTRAIT AS AGATHA CHRISTIE NOVEL
AV Bridgwood

some say the pacing drags and the ending is impossible / but I love / this solution unfurling / slowly in me like a fortune / fish in a hot palm // it all hinges on the knowledge of a child / strange / watchful / found silenced / at the birthday party with an apple in her mouth / after which violence / becomes ordinary as breakfast / (kippers sweating on a silver platter) / for the survivors / in silly hats squabbling / over an inheritance / that never existed // don't worry / I have a wise old girl in me who baffles / the authorities / by listening / to the gardener the servant the patient / raises an eyebrow at the true gent / the good wife // one day she'll gather / the squabbling selves together / ancestors looking down / from panels of oak slicked and beaten / almost into glass / and reveal who it was / who stripped / the body / who roughed up the flowerbed and slashed / grandpa's portrait / and the one / she points to will stand up / and say yes / it is I / yes / I am / the heart / of this story / yes I am / the blood of it / and I'll say O / O / I see it now / of course / that was the meaning / of the smashed clock / the unsigned letter / the figure fleeing / down the narrow passages / of the hurtling night / train to god knows where / of course / that was the Beginning / and the Middle / that led to this / finally / the Ending

ANACHRONISTIC
Emmett Coleman

Went back in time the other day and found Catullus in a sort of perpetual gilded sprawl. He had these shrewd eyes like a border terrier and in the radiance of high noon his whole lithe body seemed haloed. I couldn't stop glancing at his lips, stained as they were an almost uncanny red by sweet wine, slick and plump as rinsed strawberries, how he slipped his pen between them and it hung there with all the fierce potential of a cigarette [although of course that's not technically correct since the Romans didn't smoke cigarettes so think of something else that smoulders between the lips.]

Worked up the nerve to perch next to him and saw the bruise of Lesbia's mouth beneath the ephemera of his toga, felt about as translucent myself when I looked up to find his prying gaze already on me. *Catullus babe*, I asked, *would you consider yourself bisexual?* and he quirked a confused sort of half smile so the pen in his mouth jerked upwards and the euphemism of it all swayed in the doughy midday heat. The minutes of his silence dragged their heels [though the Romans didn't use minutes to measure time so think of something else that trickles through desperate fingers.]

Feeling vulnerable, prickling with nerves, I doubled down, asked *vos vis futuo homines aut mulieres?* and he grinned like he couldn't believe his luck or my audacity and the sun bore down like an

elevator [etc etc something else that closes distance] and he said
quod unus es? and before I could remember
if I'd ever learned the Latin for what I
am his hand was gentle but adamant
on the nape of my neck, bringing my
eager mouth towards his.

GEEZERDOM

Em Gray

Since we talked in the underpass about how to feel safe
and I impersonated the Hofmeister Bear

I've been doing him again, round the bedroom,
taking out the rubbish at night.

Not to big myself up, but I think I've mastered
the difference between teeter and swagger –

how to hold my arms banana-curved as if girthy with muscle,
invite air between my legs.

I bought a pork-pie hat –
a novelty one (but not hen-glittery)

and bear ears realistic enough. With them
I'm part me and part something else, like myth.

The Hofmeister Bear's T-shirt has his name on
which is foolish for babies and women

but I'm working up to the jacket, its yellow holler,
the neon flash of *Follow The Bear*

for when being followed means you're the boss.

SEAHORSE GRAMMAR: CYDIPPE

Michelle Szobody

I like a man whose body is a question mark —
a thousand answers wait inside my swollen belly.

I like a man whose body opens like a pair of brackets —
my swollen belly ready to fill the blank inside his brood pouch.

I like a man who can hold a complex syntax —
the full stops of my eggs find his wriggly commas,

embed into his womb, make him a man
whose belly swells more than mine ever could.

I watch while he delivers our young.
Their gorgeous semicolon-shapes scrawl the current

like hundreds of little hinges in the sentence of our love,
saying, *we are this; also this;*

these; that;
this too; those;

DIARY OF A FRONTIER BRIDE

Rebecca Ferrier

If I write you on horseback, I am the horse:
the ridden thing / a software of flesh / a waiting malfunction in a bridle.

entry #05

    I met a logger man in the copse beside our farmhouse
    who said there were no trees worth cutting down
    and wouldn't be until he died. He has a son, though,
    who'll return when there's wood here.

    I have plans for the wood-in-waiting,
    as he has plans for his son.

If I write you coming home, I am the home:
the table, your chair / dressed nicely / a comely scent.

entry #19

    I kindle pastoral fantasies with the eggs in the pantry,
    though never any chickens to lay them.
    As though poultry would make us too real
    and my wishes an untimely knock on the door by your Stetson.

    I've been collecting the clothes I think you'd want me
    to take off, to complement what I imagine you'd wear.

If I write you married, I am the Mrs:
the ridden thing / a software of flesh / a waiting malfunction in a bride.

entry #37

    I fear I am not young enough to bend;
    that I waited too long and there's no flesh here to pair,
    only pulp for jam or cider. You could choose from many wives

and their horses and a farm with a copse to the east, facing dawn.

entry #68

entry #112

entry #901

When the logger man's son appears, he finds a ruin and takes the gowns I'd keep as tinder: all I made of the years.

WATER TORTURE
Marcia Hindson

Somewhere, a woman moves five hundred
and eighty three days closer to her wedding night
although she's not aware of that yet.

And once I had a heart so wild a whole
continent had to reintroduce the hunting of wolves
to stop it haemorrhaging and howling everywhere.

In the house of adolescence, someone's kid brother
just asked the flocked wallpaper what a hard on is
and a spider plant wick with spiderettes laughs.

I've been running these streets the way
salmon run rivers for decades now and still
I don't know the true depth of my shadow.

My next door neighbour has become
a paid up supporter of broken wine bottles
neglected in overgrown communal corners.

In the films that play in my head, love is always a fist
with sticky, goggly eyes attached even when it is
a whole meadow of people just walking away on repeat.

When nostalgia laces up its Doc Martens
I hide every one of my anxieties in the attic
until it decides it's ready to clop off again.

My mother once thought about burning down
the house but the idea of all the murdered moths
made her throw three boxes of matches away.

I used to be the kind of person that fucked reluctant
men in lakes as it rained. Now the kind of fucking
I do involves the subterranean chasms of my head.

And I have never met a bird that is mad
to this day although I've walked enough
thunderstorms in search of a trace of one.

My longing has been haunting
the bathroom plughole for months now
so the cold water tap is terrified of dripping.

Another lonely rat was shot from the smashed
kitchen window of number seven this morning.
Confessions can explode as distant as Polaris.

Don't steal my telescope next time you decide
the stars have aligned for another leaving.

CONTRIBUTORS

SANAH AHSAN is a poet, liberation psychologist, writer and educator. Sanah won the Out-Spoken Poetry Performance Prize 2019, was shortlisted for the Queen Mary New Writing Prize 2022, White Review Poet's Prize 2021, and Bridport Poetry Prize 2021. Their poetry has been featured on Channel 4 and BBC, and published or forthcoming in *Wasafiri*, *Poetry Wales*, *The White Review*, *Ink Sweat & Tears*, *fourteen poems* and anthologised by presses like Pan-Macmillan. Sanah was the poet and lyricist for a theatre adaptation of *The Jungle Book*. Sanah is currently writing their debut poetry collection, exploring queerness, Islam and intergenerational trauma.

MARTHA AROHA ЧЕЛОК is an emerging poet. Published by the London Wildlife Trust and *takahē magazine*, they are interested in how ecopoetics responds to human anxieties, including (dis)ability, growing pains, identity and belonging. They live with takiwātanga and aroreretini (autism and ADHD), and owe their reo and ao Māori to the London whānau, Ngāti Rānana.

ISABELLE BAAFI is the Reviews Editor at *Poetry London*. Her pamphlet *Ripe* (ignitionpress, 2020) won a Somerset Maugham Award and was a Poetry Book Society Pamphlet Choice.

TOM BAILEY is a poet based in Edinburgh. His poems have been published in magazines including *The Poetry Review*, *berlin lit*, *bath magg*, *Propel Magazine*, *Anthropocene*, *Under the Radar*, *The North*, and *Poetry News*. He also edits the online poetry magazine and archive *And Other Poems*.

DEBMALYA BANDYOPADHYAY is a writer and mathematician based in Birmingham, UK. His poems, translations, and essays have appeared or are forthcoming in *Ghost City Review*, *LEON Literary Review*, *Couplet Poetry*, *Ballast*, *On Eating*, and *Anthropocene Poetry*, among other literary journals. His work has been selected for the *Yearbook of Indian Poetry in English* (2023) and he was a finalist for SweetLit's 2024 Poetry Prize. He can often be found in parks confabulating with local birds.

GEMMA BARNETT is a poet, writer and actor. She won the 'Poetry for Good' Prize/BBC Words First in 2021. Her poem 'My Abortion was Funny' was published in the Verve Poetry Festival *Anthology on Protest* and commended for the Out-Spoken Poetry Prize 2023. Other published work can be found in *AUB International Poetry Prize Anthology* and *Anthropocene*.

CLÍODHNA BHREATNACH is from Waterford. She was Highly Commended for the Forward Prize for Best Poem in 2022 and the recipient of Arts Council Agility Awards in 2021 and 2022. Her poetry has appeared in *Banshee Magazine*, *Abridged*, the Dedalus Press anthology *Local Wonders*, and *The Forward Book of Poetry 2023*.

IAIN BLEAKLEY is a poet and dancer originally from Edinburgh who resides in London. He has had poems commissioned for Worldwide FM and Loose FM and work published in *The Rialto*, *Ink Cypher* and *The ghost furniture catalogue*. In his spare time he enjoys rolling around the floor and rearranging supermarket receipts.

NATALIE LINH BOLDERSTON is a Vietnamese-Chinese-British poet. In 2020, she received an Eric Gregory Award and co-won the Rebecca Swift Women Poets' Prize. Her poem 'Middle Name with Diacritics' came third in the 2019 National Poetry Competition and was shortlisted for the 2021 Forward Prize for Best Single Poem. Her pamphlet, *The Protection of Ghosts*, was published by V. Press in 2019. She is now working on her first full-length collection.

JO BRATTEN's debut pamphlet, *Climacteric*, was published in 2022 by Fly on the Wall. Her work has been published in *And Other Poems*, *Bad Lilies*, *berlin lit*, *The Interpreter's House*, *The London Magazine*, *Poetry*

Birmingham Literary Journal, Poetry London, Poetry Wales and *The Rialto*, amongst others. She lives in London.

FRANCESCA BROOKS is a writer and researcher, living and working in Manchester. Francesca's poetry and essays have been published with *PN Review, gorse, Tentacular* and *3AM Magazine*, amongst others. Her book about the Anglo-Welsh, poet-artist David Jones, *Poet of the Medieval Modern: Reading the Early Medieval Library with David Jones*, won the University English Book Prize 2022. In a previous life, Francesca worked with art galleries, rare book dealers, frozen food companies and even a circus.

RACHEL BRUCE (she/her) is a poet based in South London. Her work has appeared in *The Poetry Review, Propel Magazine, Mslexia, Ink Sweat & Tears, The Telegraph*, and *Atrium*, among others.

AV BRIDGWOOD is a writer from Manchester. They are a former Foyle Young Poet and recent graduate of UEA's MA Poetry. AV was commended in the National Poetry Competition 2023. Their work is published in journals such as *Magma* (forthcoming), *The Interpreter's House*, and *Lighthouse*.

CASPAR BRYANT is a poet from west Cornwall. Caspar's work was shortlisted for the 2023 Oxford Poetry Prize and can be found in *SPAM zine, The Alchemy Spoon, And Other Poems, Banshee*, Broken Sleep's *Modern Poetries 1*, and elsewhere.

NATALIE BURDETT was born in the West Midlands. Her creative writing PhD thesis investigates the poetry of urban place. Her poems have appeared in several anthologies and magazines and been shortlisted for the London Magazine and Bridport prizes. Her Laureate's Choice pamphlet, *Urban Drift*, was published by smith|doorstop in 2018.

SHANI CADWALLENDER is a queer, working-class, 'mixed-race' woman from Northeast England who currently lives in London. She teaches English, writes poetry and is studying part-time towards a CHASE-funded PhD at Birkbeck UoL. This creative-critical project is about trees and identity in the poetry of three 'marginal' nineteenth-century women poets, linking their works to contemporary ecopoetics through creative interventions. She has been published by *Dreich*, *Ink, Sweat & Tears*, and the 87 Press' magazine, *The Hythe*, amongst others.

MAYA CASPARI is a writer and academic. Her research focuses on the ethics of representing difficult histories. Her poetry has been published in journals including *The Poetry Review*, *Ambit*, *Butcher's Dog* and *Perverse*. She has been highly commended in the Forward Prizes, longlisted in the National Poetry Competition and shortlisted for the Aesthetica Creative Writing Award.

KARAN CHAMBERS (she/her) is a poet, tutor, and former English teacher. She has a degree in Creative Writing from UEA and is about to start an MA in Creative Writing (Poetry) at Royal Holloway. She has poems in *Butcher's Dog*, *Gutter*, *Mslexia*, and *Propel Magazine*. Karan was awarded Highly Commended in the 2023 Cheltenham Poetry Competition, and Runner-Up in the 2024 Classical Association Poetry Competition. Her debut pamphlet *woman | folk* is forthcoming in 2024.

STUART CHARLESWORTH is a working class, non-binary poet and nurse, working in Mental Health services. They were shortlisted in the 2021 Live Canon poetry competition and in the 2020 Rialto pamphlet competition. They were commended in the 2018 Brittle Star competition and the 2021 Hippocrates prize. Stuart has an MA in creative writing (UEA) and helps run *Café Writers*.

ALANA CHASE is an American poet and editor based in London. Her poems are featured in *berlin lit*, *Fish Barrel Review*, *Full House Literary*, and elsewhere.

CIA is a poet and student from London.

ADAM CLIFFORD is an actor, theatre-maker, composer and writer. He received a grant from Arts Council England to develop his practice as a poet.

COGWHEEL is an artist, writer and songwriter who currently lives (and grew up) in the rural outskirts of Stoke-on-Trent. With uncounted years' experience of chronically successful hoarding, Cogwheel continues to live life as somewhat of a recluse, sporadically performing and continually collecting, making things, attempting to capture fleeting and sometimes festering thoughts with words and song.

EMMETT COLEMAN lives in Scotland and writes poems from time to time, about being queer and about being alive.

JARED COLLINS is a poet from West Berkshire, writing poetry and songs in his free time. He graduated with a BA in English with Creative Writing from Goldsmiths, University of London in 2020. He is also a self-taught painter.

KATHERINE COLLINS's poems have appeared in *The Rialto*, *bath magg*, *Shearsman Magazine*, and *Finished Creatures*, among others. In 2022, her collaboration with composer Christopher Cook won the Rosamond Prize and in 2023 she was highly commended in the Plough Prize.

CLAIRE COLLISON, artist and writer, was one of three winners of the inaugural Women Poets' Prize, 2018. She was Highly Commended in the Gingko Prize, 2023 and was placed second in Resurgence Prize, 2014; Hippocrates Prize, 2017; and Winchester Poetry Prize, 2020. Her poetry is included in anthologies, including *Second Place Rosette: Poems about Britain* (Emma Press), *The Valley Press Anthology of Prose Poetry*, and *Field Notes on Survival* (Bad Betty Press) and can be found online and in magazines, including *Perverse*, *Corrupted Poets*, *Magma*, *Butcher's Dog*, *Finished Creatures*, and *The Rialto*. She is a founder member of Poets for the Planet. Her debut pamphlet, *Placebo*, is published by Blueprint.

LEYLA ÇOLPAN is a poet and translator based in London, UK and Pittsburgh, PA. Hir work has been awarded an Academy of American Poets Undergraduate Prize and the 2020 Gulf Coast Prize for Poetry, and it has been published in *The Adroit Journal*, *Magma Poetry*, and *Best New Poets*. Ze received hir MA from Goldsmiths, University of London in 2023.

COURTNEY CONRAD is a Jamaican poet. Her debut pamphlet *I Am Evidence* is published by Bloodaxe Books. She is a winner of the Eric Gregory Award, Michael Marks Award, Bridport Prize Young Writers Award and Mslexia Women's Pamphlet Prize. Shortlisted for The White Review Poet's Prize, the Manchester Poetry Prize, the Oxford Brookes International Poetry Competition, the Aesthetica Creative Writing Award's Poetry Prize, the Bridport Poetry Prize, Derby Poetry Festival Poetry Prize and the Poetry Wales Pamphlet competition. She has been published widely and is a Cave Canem fellow.

SILAS CURTIS is is a support worker and poet based in Glasgow. He has published with *Wet Grain*, *Ink Sweat & Tears*, *Abridged*, and *Osmosis*.

RACHEL CURZON received an Eric Gregory Award in 2007, and her debut pamphlet was published in 2016 under the Faber New Poets scheme. Other work has appeared in *The Rialto*, *Magma*, *Tangerine*, the *Bridport Anthology* and *The Tree Line: Poems for Woods, Trees & People*, edited by Michael McKimm. Rachel was born in Leeds, had a long stint in Hampshire, and now lives in North Yorkshire.

IULIA DAVID is a Romanian-born London-based poet whose first pamphlet, *Blueprint*, was published in 2022 by Green Bottle Press. She is currently working on her first collection.

DIDE is an award-winning poet, painter and composer-musician based in East Anglia. Her debut poetry pamphlet, *Growing*, was published by Broken Sleep Books in March 2022 and her debut poetry collection, *Making Sense*, by Verve Poetry Press in April 2023.

BETTY DOYLE is a disabled poet from Merseyside, where she works at a sixth form college. Her work has appeared in publications such as *Agenda*, *Butcher's Dog*, *The North*, and *Poetry Wales*. She has a PhD in Creative Writing from Manchester Metropolitan University, where she researched infertility poetics. Her debut poetry pamphlet, *Girl Parts*, was published by Verve Poetry Press in 2022. Her upcoming pamphlet, *Fruits of Labour*, will be published by Seren in October 2024.

AMY DUGMORE is a poet and copywriter from Birmingham, UK. Her poems have appeared in *Atrium*, *The Madrigal* and *Under My Pillow* anthology.

SHAKEEMA EDWARDS is an Antiguan American writer living in Belfast. She has received an Ireland Chair of Poetry Student Award and was shortlisted for the 2023 Manchester Poetry Prize. Her work has appeared in *Magma*, *Poetry Ireland Review*, *New Isles Press*, *Channel*, and *The Apiary*.

CHLOE ELLIOTT is a poet based in the North. She is a winner of the 2022 New Poets Prize as well as the 2020 Creative Future Writers' Award. Her writing features in *Poetry Birmingham Literary Journal*, *bath magg*, *Bedtime Stories for the End of the World*, *The North*, *Magma* and *Strix* amongst others.

EVE ELLIS is an American poet and educator living in London. Her debut pamphlet is forthcoming from ignitionpress in 2024.

KRISTIAN EVANS is a Welsh poet and editor, interested in ecological philosophy, animism and the history of magic. He has written several texts for performance, a chapbook of poems, *Unleaving* (HappenStance

2015) and *Otherworlds* a chapbook of non-fiction (with Zoë Brigley; Broken Sleep, 2021). He is the founding editor of *MODRON*, funded by a New Audiences Grant from Books Council of Wales. He is co-editor of the poetry anthology *100 Poems to Save the Earth*, and he edited the Dwelling issue of *Magma Poetry* with Brigley and Rob A. Mackenzie. He was the judge for the poetry award of the Wales Book of the Year 2023.

TITILAYO FARUKUOYE is a writer, educator and organiser based in Glasgow. Titilayo co-directs the Scottish BPOC Writers Network and is a co-winner of the 2022 Edwin Morgan Poetry Award. Titilayo's poetry featured at Fringe of Colour, Edinburgh Multicultural Festival and Paisley Book Festival and *Our Time is A Garden Anthology* among others.

IRUM FAZAL is a writer whose work has been performed at Wigmore Hall and the Southbank Centre, and published by independent presses, including Earthbound Press and Face Press. She was formerly a visiting artist to the Judith E. Wilson drama studio in Cambridge and is Artistic Director of ONCE arts.

MAVE FELLOWES is the author of *Chaplin & Company* (Cape, 2013). Her writing has appeared in *Poetry Birmingham Literary Journal*, Granta's *New Voices*, *The Paris Review Daily*, *Stand*, and *blunt instrument*, a limited edition book by the artist Mary Ramsden. She is currently on the second year of a part-time MA in Writing Poetry with The Poetry School/University of Newcastle.

REBECCA FERRIER's debut novel *The Salt Bind* is due for publication by Renegade in 2025. She is pursuing a Creative Writing PhD at Northumbria University, having been awarded a fully-funded studentship. She previously won the Bridge Award and was shortlisted for the Alpine Fellowship Poetry Prize in 2023 and 2024.

DEBORAH FINDING is a queer feminist writer with a background in academia and activism. Her publications include *fourteen poems*, *The Friday Poem* and *berlin lit*. She is widely anthologised, and her debut pamphlet, *vigils for dead and dying girls*, is out now with Nine Pens. She won the the Write By The Sea single poem prize, the Live Canon competition for her forthcoming pamphlet, 'amortisation', and has been shortlisted or commended for the Troubadour, Live Canon, Hexham, Hammond House, and Ver Poets Prizes. She is poet in residence at London's Soho Poly Theatre.

ALI FITZPATRICK is a London-based writer of mixed British-Asian heritage. A recent graduate from SOAS with an MA in History of Art and Architecture of the Islamic Middle East, her poetry explores themes of self, food and religion. She's trying to find a way to capture that feeling of being in between. Her work was first published in late 2022 in *t'ART magazine*.

LIVIA FRANCHINI is a writer & translator from Tuscany, Italy. She is the author of a novel, *Shelf Life* (Doubleday, 2019) and a poetry pamphlet, *Our Available Magic* (Makina Books, 2019). Her latest English-language translation is *The Sky is Falling* by Lorenza Mazzetti (Another Gaze Publications, 2023) and a second novel is slated for publication by Doubleday in 2024. Livia is Lecturer in Creative Writing at Goldsmiths where she also coordinates The Goldsmiths Prize for innovative fiction. With Lucy Mercer, she co-edits *TOO LITTLE/TOO HARD*, a magazine on the intersections of work, time and value. She lives in London.

OLIVE FRANKLIN is a poet based in London. Her poetry has previously been published by 87Press online, Foyle's Young Poet Award and she has given a reading for Inkandescent's BOLD. She runs an LGBT+ women's poetry group that meets on the Southbank and works at The Poetry Society.

MIRUNA FULGEANU is a Romanian-born poet and translator based in London. Her work has appeared in *Poetry London*, *The Yale Review*, *perverse*, *The Rialto*, *berlin lit* and *Pain* among others. She is the winner of the 2023 Oxford Poetry Prize, and is currently working on her debut collection with the support of the Prototype Development Programme.

SAM FURLONG lives in Dublin. In 2023, they completed an MA in Poetry at the Seamus Heaney Centre, where they were awarded the Ireland Chair of Poetry Student Prize. Their poems appear or are forthcoming in *Banshee*, *Catflap*, *Sonder*, *Poetry Ireland Review* and elsewhere. They were selected for *Poetry Ireland's Introductions* by Tara Bergin.

CHARLOTTE GEATER is a poet who lives in Walthamstow. They won the White Review Poets' Prize in 2018 and have been published in *SPAMzine*, *Clinic*, and *Strange Horizons*. They have published pamphlets with Bad Betty Press, if a leaf falls press, and Legitimate Snack.

YANITA GEORGIEVA is a poet and journalist. Her debut pamphlet, *Small Undetectable Thefts*, received the Eric Gregory Prize. She is an alum of the Southbank New Poets Collective and the London Library Emerging Writers Scheme. She was born in Bulgaria, raised in Lebanon, and now lives in London.

AYSAR GHASSAN lives in Coventry and was a 'core poet' at BBC Contains Strong Language, 2021. His poems feature in journals including *Poetry Wales*, *Under The Radar*, *Ambit*, *Magma*, *The Interpreter's House*, *Poetry Birmingham Literary Journal*, *The Lampeter Review* and *Strix*. In addition, they have been broadcast on BBC 6 Music and 5 Live. Aysar teaches Automotive & Transport Design and in 2021 he wrote and narrated a talk on Automotive Design for the BBC programme 'The Essay'. In 2022 he was a Room 204 mentee with Writing West Midlands.

EM GRAY is a neurodivergent poet living in Brighton. She has been highly commended by the Forward Prizes, won second prize in the Mslexia Poetry Competition and been shortlisted for the Creative Future Writers' Award.

KAREN GREEN has been writing poems for many years. She has done many courses, entered several competitions (her best result was a highly commended in the Bridport Prize judged by Mimi Khalvati). She is trying to place her poems in magazines as this seems to be a good way forward.

MILLIE GUILLE is a writer and editor based in London, and holds an MSt in Creative Writing from the University of Oxford. Her poetry has been longlisted for the National Poetry Competition and the 2023 Mslexia Poetry Competition, and she was a prizewinner in the 2024 Magma Poetry Prize. Her work has appeared in *Propel Magazine*, *Bad Lilies*, and *Magma* Issue 89, and she is currently working on her debut poetry collection.

ELONTRA HALL is a Black American poet and educator living in Northampton, England. His work focuses on art, basketball and fatherhood among other things. His poetry has been published in *HeadFake*, *Butcher's Dog* (16) and *Magma* (82). He has also had his work broadcast on BBC 4's *Poetry Please* (Christmas 2022). He is an Obsidian Fellow and a member of the inaugural Griot's Well cohort.

ADAM HEARDMAN is a poet and writer from Newcastle upon Tyne. His poems have appeared in *PN Review*, *The Rialto*, *The North*, *MOTH*, *PAIN Journal*, a Broken Sleep anthology about Aphex Twin, and other places. He has worked with several visual artists and writes art criticism regularly for *Art Monthly* magazine. He currently lives and works in East London.

ERICA HESKETH's poems have appeared in *The North*, *Magma*, *harana poetry* and *PERVERSE* among others. She placed second in the 2022

Winchester Poetry Prize, was commended in the 2023 Magma Poetry Competition and the 2023 Stanza Competition, and was longlisted in the 2024 National Poetry Competition. She is a member of the Southbank Centre New Poets Collective 2023–24.

LOU HILL is a poet, musician, carpenter. His poems have been published in *The Poetry Review*, *Swerve Magazine*, *Grass Mag*, and *Ink, Sweat & Tears*. His most recent spoken-word record 'Dogends' featured on *The Late Junction* (BBCR3), *Tom Robinson's Introducing Mixtape* (BBCR6), and BBC Radio London.

MARCIA HINDSON is a working class writer from the Northeast of England. Her work has appeared in *Magma*, *The Interpreter's House*, *Obsessed With Pipework*, *Tears In The Fence*, and others. She loves moss and clouds, and considers herself a proud weirdling. She is currently working on her first collection.

JULIA IRELAND is a queer gardener who is preoccupied with death. She is a death doula in training in order to put this preoccupation to good use. She loves cats, acknowledges that this a lesbian cliché and is working toward her first poetry collection.

IAN IRWIN was selected as an Out-Spoken Press Emerging Poet in 2022 and his poetry has been published in *The Poetry Review*, *Propel Magazine*, *berlin lit*, *Carmen et Error*, *The Alchemy Spoon* and *Trasna* among others. He lives and works in Bristol.

ALEX JENKINS is a writer and civil servant who lives in London. His poetry has been published in *Bad Lilies* and elsewhere. He is finishing his first pamphlet, which explores religious faith and its loss, parenthood, and lyrebirds.

EWAN JOHN (He/Him) is a queer engineering student originally from Cardiff. He can usually be found sitting during his lectures writing film reviews on Letterboxd.

CAITLIN TINA JONES is an emerging poet from Hengoed, South Wales. She is currently studying towards her BA in Creative Writing at Cardiff University. Her poems have featured in publications by Pan Macmillan and Lucent Dreaming, and her poetry reviews have featured in publications by the Institute of Welsh Affairs.

FIN KEEGAN: Dubliner Fin Keegan lives with his family in the West of Ireland, where he works as a book editor. Recent poems appear in *Channel, Howl, Drawn to the Light Press, Cold Mountain Review* and the *Amsterdam Quarterly*.

SHAYNA KOWALCZYK is an Indian-Mauritian-Polish poet and writer from South London. She is a member of the Roundhouse Poetry Collective 22–23.

DOMINIC LEONARD's writing can be found in *The Poetry Review, Poetry London, PN Review, Pain*, the *TLS*, and elsewhere. In 2019 he won an Eric Gregory Award, and in 2022 he won the Oxford Poetry Prize. He lives and teaches in London.

LUCILLE MONA LING is a poet from Berlin, currently based in Glasgow. Her poetry has been published in *The Dark Horse, Gutter, Horizon Magazine*, and *Middleground Magazine*. She has been included in the Scottish Poetry Library Anthology of *Best Scottish Poems of 2021*. Since 2023 she is the founder and poetry editor at *Contralytic* an interdisciplinary philosophy journal.

SIMON MADDRELL's poems have appeared in numerous publications including *Acumen, AMBIT, Butcher's Dog, Magma, Poetry Wales, Propel Magazine, Stand, The Gay & Lesbian Review, The Moth, The Rialto, Under the Radar*. In 2020, Queerfella jointly-won The Rialto Open Pamphlet Competition. *Isle of Sin* (Polari Press, 2023), *The Whole Island* (Valley Press, 2023), and *a finger in derek jarman's mouth* (Polari Press, 2024) were all Poetry Book Society Pamphlet Selections.

CIARA MAGUIRE is a writer based in Glasgow. Her writing has been published in *Gutter*, *Extra Teeth*, *bath magg*, *SPAM zine* and more. Her debut pamphlet, *Impossible Heat*, was published this summer with Little Betty Press.

AGATA MASLOWSKA is a poet, writer, and translator born in Poland and living in Scotland. Her poetry and fiction have appeared in various magazines, including *Edinburgh Review*, *New Writing Scotland*, *Gutter*, *Magma*, *Blackbox Manifold*, *The Interpreter's House*, *amberflora*, *Tentacular*, and in several anthologies, including *Glasgow* (Dostoyevsky Wannabe, 2022) and *Footprints: Ecopoetry Anthology* (Broken Sleep Books, 2022). She is the recipient of the Scottish Book Trust New Writers Award, the Hawthornden Writing Fellowship, and the Gillian Purvis Award for New Writing.

REBECCA MCCUTCHEON is a poet working on the Essex coast. Her work has been published in *The Poetry Review* and *berlin lit*. Her debut collection, *Down*, is published by Out-Spoken Press.

TRACEY MCEVOY is a poet, writer and editor. She graduated with Distinction from the Master's in Creative Writing from Kent University in 2023. Her work has been published in *Propel Magazine*, *Poetry Wales*, *Feast*, and *Grindstone*. In 2024, she was shortlisted in the Alpine Fellowship Poetry Prize and the London Library Emerging Writer Programme.

MEGAN MCKIE-SMITH is a writer and audio describer from Newcastle. She's currently working on her debut pamphlet.

TOM MCLAUGHLIN is a London-based Northern Irish poet. He completed an MA in Creative Writing, with Distinction, at Royal Holloway University and is now undertaking a practice-based PhD at Surrey University on queer domestic space. His poetry pamphlet *Open Houses* was published in 2021 by Marble Press. His poems have featured in publications such as MMU's *Write Where We Are Now*, *Porridge Magazine*, *Alchemy Spoon*, and *Channel Magazine*.

RAFAEL MENDES is a Brazilian migrant based in Ireland. His work is upcoming in *Poetry Ireland Review* and *Poetry Salzburg Review*. He has been selected for Poetry Ireland's 2023 Introduction Series and was awarded the Irish Writers Centre/Tyrone Guthrie Centre Lacuna Bursary 2023. His poem 'On Failure and Persistence' was selected for Poetry Day Ireland 2024.

JON ALEX MILLER (he, him) lives in London with his husband and dog. He has poems published in *Acumen*, *Acropolis*, *Atrium* and *Magma*. He works with big businesses on climate change and social justice.

NATALIE MOORES is a poet from Manchester living and working in London. She won the Overton Poetry prize in 2018 with her debut pamphlet collection, *Single Girl Lies Hidden*, published shortly after. She has been featured in publications including *Shooter Literary Magazine*, *Ink, Sweat & Tears*, *Coronaverses Collective*, *Best of Manchester Poets*, *Medusa's Laugh Press* (USA) and many more. She's also a keen spoken word performer and workshop facilitator alongside the day job of running her own branding studio.

EIRA ELISABETH MURPHY is 22 and from Liverpool. She is a previous winner of the Foyle Young Poets of the Year Award and has been published in *Banshee Magazine*.

FRANCIS-XAVIER MUKIIBI is a poet of Ugandan heritage from North London. He is an alumnus of the Barbican Young Poets programme, the Roundhouse Poetry Collective and the Obsidian Foundation retreat. He was the recipient of an Eric Gregory Award in 2024. His poems appear in *Under the Radar*, *Poetry Wales*, *Magma* and *Poetry London* among others.

THEMBE MVULA is a South African/British writer and poet, an alum of the Obsidian Foundation retreat, Barbican Young Poets and the Roundhouse Poetry Collective. Her poetry has been recently anthologised in *Part of a Story That Started Before Me* (Penguin Random House, 2023), *Before Them, We* (Flipped Eye Publishing, 2022), *The Black Anthology* (10:10 Press, 2021) and appears in *Magma* magazine issues 77 and 83.

DAVID NASH, born 1985, is a poet and translator from County Cork. His pamphlet, *The Islands of Chile,* came out in 2022 with fourteen poems, and his first full collection, *No Man's Land*, was published by Dedalus Press in 2023. The latter won the Seamus Heaney Prize in 2024, and was shortlisted for the Ondaatje Prize and the Listowel Pigott Prize. He lives between Ireland and Chile.

JACKSON PHOENIX NASH (he/him) is a queer transgender poet and teacher from Essex. His work has appeared in *Propel Magazine*, *Rattle*, *Channel*, *Baffling Magazine* and many more. His debut pamphlet, *Some People are Trains*, was published by Little Betty in 2024.

SERGE ♆ NEPTUNE has been called 'the little merman of British poetry'. He is a Faber Academy alumnus and a queer neuro-divergent poet based in London. His work has been placed in the National Poetry Competition and the Winchester Poetry Competition. Several poems appeared in *bath magg, Propel Magazine, The North, The Rialto, Banshee, Magma,* and elsewhere. His latest pamphlet, *Mother Night*, is published by the Emma Press.

YAZ NIN is a Kibris born, London based poet and playwright. Her poems have been featured in *Oxford Poetry, 14, The other side of hope, Passionfruit Review* (online) and *Dust* (online). Her poem 'falling out of rituals' was performed at the Arcola Theatre (part of a fundraiser for charity).

S. NIROSHINI is a London-based writer. Her poetry pamphlet *Darling Girl* was published in 2021 by Bad Betty Press and three of her poems were included in the recent Bloodaxe anthology *Out of Sri Lanka*.

RICHARD O'BRIEN's publications include *A Bloody Mess* (Valley Press, 2015) and *The Dolphin House* (Broken Sleep, 2021), as well as work in a range of magazines and anthologies including *The Poetry Review* and *The White Review*. He won an Eric Gregory Award from the Society of Authors in 2017, and is an Assistant Professor in Creative Writing at Northumbria University. He was the Birmingham Poet Laureate 2018–2020. Richard is currently working on a novel and an experimental music memoir about the American band the Mountain Goats.

PATRICK O'DONOGHUE is a journalist and writer living in Dublin. He works for *The Sunday Times* in Ireland. His poetry has previously featured in *The Honest Ulsterman* and *Wordlegs*.

EUGENE O'HARE is an Irish author & actor. He was recently shortlisted for the poetry prize at Belfast Book Festival, and the Fish Poetry Prize. He is working towards a first collection. Recent poems appear in *Stand, Causeway, Cyphers* and more.

OLUWASEUN (SEUN) OLAYIWOLA is a poet, choreographer, and critic based in London. His work has been published *The Guardian, The Poetry Review, Poetry London*, the *TLS* and elsewhere. His debut collection is forthcoming from Fitzcarraldo Editions (UK) and Soft Skull Press (US).

BEN PHILIPPS is a critic and poet from London. The winner of the 2024 Telegraph Poetry prize, he's also a Clarendon Scholar at the University of Oxford, and writes widely on modern and contemporary literature.

ALEX PRIESTLEY is a writer from Leeds, UK, currently based in York. Some of his recent work has appeared or is forthcoming in *La Piccioletta Barca*, *Spectra Poets*, and *Poetry Online*.

ZAHRA RAFIQ is a seventeen-year-old poet studying for her A-levels in Chemistry, Biology, Physics and Maths. She is a winner of the Foyle Young Poets of the Year award 2022, and enjoys incorporating science into her work. She seeks poetic inspiration in nature, and by the age of eleven had scaled the three highest peaks in the United Kingdom.

TAZ RAHMAN is a Cardiff based poet, writer and literary content creator. He has been published in *Poetry Wales*, *Bad Lilies*, *South Bank Poetry*, *Anthropocene*, *Honest Ulsterman*, *Nation Cymru*, *Culture Matters* and various anthologies. He has been selected to be the Chairperson of Poetry Wales Magazine's Readers' Committee from September 2022 and is editor of the climate emergency themed literary journal *Modron* alongside poets Zoë Brigley and Kristian Evans. He was one of the judges for the 2021 Poetry Wales Pamphlet Competition. In 2021 he was awarded a place in the Literature Wales writer development programme Representing Wales, and was mentored by Zoë Brigley. He founded the Youtube poetry channel 'Just Another Poet' in 2019, which is presently supported by the Books Council Wales and had previously received literary commissions from Literature Wales. His debut collection *East of the Sun, West of the Moon* was published by Seren Books in 2024.

MOHAMMAD S. RAZAI was born in Kabul in the winter of 1986 and moved to Britain at the age of fourteen as a child refugee. He studied medicine at the University of Cambridge and now works as a doctor in the NHS. He is a lecturer and researcher at the University of Cambridge. His poems have been published in *Brittle Stars*, *Tears in the Fence*, *The Poetry Review*, *Under the Radar*, and the *Brixton Review of Books*.

MUSKAAN RAZDAN is an Indian poet/ creative based in London. She's an alumna of the Roundhouse Poetry Collective and the Apple and Snakes Writers Room. Her work has been published in *Magma, berlin lit, The Cardiff Review* and *Propel Magazine*. She has also been published in several anthologies in India and the UK.

LUCIE RICHTER-MAHR grew up in Berlin and currently lives between London and Yorkshire. She is interested in the poetics of translation and conservation and has previously held residencies at two literary archives. Her poems appeared in *Footprints: an anthology of new ecopoetry* by Broken Sleep Books and are forthcoming in *Lighthouse*.

ZAIN RISHI is a British Indian writer and bookseller from Birmingham, currently based in Edinburgh. His writing has featured in *Gutter, Honeycomb Press, The Inkwell, From Arthur's Seat* and *The Oxford Student*. He is currently working on his debut poetry pamphlet, exploring how language is related to bodies, identity and intimacy.

MARK SAUNDERS lives on the Isle of Wight in the UK. His poetry can be found in *Abridged, The Alchemy Spoon, The Cannon's Mouth, Confluence, The Interpreter's House, Magma, Meniscus, The Museum of Americana, Red Ogre, Soft Star, Spelt* and *Strix*. He has read at Ventnor Fringe Festival and other venues.

MARINA SCOTT grew up predominantly in the water on the beach in Falmouth, Cornwall. They are currently completing an MA in Creative & Life Writing at Goldsmiths, where they're thinking about the Anthropocene, queerness and hydrofeminism through poetics. They work for a literary festival and co-run a community poetry night in SE London, Resonance, which fundraises for local mutual aid groups. They've published with Broken Sleep Books (*Cornish Modern Poetries*, 2022), *SPAM Zine, Lucy Writers Platform, Antithesis Journal*, and *Sticky Fingers*, among others. Marina's first pamphlet, *Lips Blue, Drying Up*, is forthcoming from Death of Workers Press.

JP SEABRIGHT is a queer disabled writer living in London. They have four solo pamphlets published and two collaborations, encompassing poetry, prose and experimental work. They explore themes of gender, sexuality, trauma and the climate crisis in their work. This poem is inspired by a series of misreadings that Anthony Vahni posted on their (now deleted) Twitter account.

ANNA SHELTON is a teacher and writer from Cambridge. Her poem 'Black Fen' inspired her first folk song, which she performed at the 2022 Cambridge Folk Festival. She has been published in *Coven*, *Streetcake* magazine and the 2024 Sidhe Press anthology *To Light the Trails – Poems By Women In A Violent World*. She was commended in the Hippocrates prize 2024. She is currently writing her first pamphlet, which was longlisted for Verve in 2023.

HENRY ST LEGER (he/they) is a poet, journalist and Cambridge literature graduate who has appeared in *Propel Magazine*, *Poetry London*, *Magma*, and Broken Sleep's *Masculinity: An Anthology of Modern Voices*. Their writing takes inspiration from the news cycle and the power of language to assert or subvert the status quo.

PAUL STEPHENSON studied modern languages and linguistics. He has published three pamphlets: *Those People* (Smith/Doorstop, 2015), which won the Poetry Business pamphlet competition; *The Days that Followed Paris* (HappenStance, 2016), written after the November 2015 terrorist attacks; and *Selfie with Waterlilies* (Paper Swans Press, 2017). In 2013/14 he took part in the Jerwood/Arvon mentoring scheme and the Aldeburgh Eight, before completing an MA in Creative Writing (Poetry) with the Manchester Writing School. In 2018 he co-edited the 'Europe' issue of *Magma* (70) and currently co-curates Poetry in Aldeburgh. His first collection will be published by Carcanet in 2023.

ELLORA SUTTON is a prize-winning poet based in Hampshire. Her work has been published in *The Poetry Review*, *berlin lit*, and *Banshee*, among others, and she is the poetry reviewer for *Mslexia*. Her pamphlets include *Artisanal Slush* (Verve Poetry Press) and *Antonyms for Burial* (fourteen poems), the latter of which was the Poetry Book Society Spring 2023 Pamphlet Choice.

MICHELLE SZOBODY is a British-American poet, translator, and researcher based in Brighton, whose work explores women and relationships in literature. She is the recipient of a DYCP grant, and her children's adaptation of Beowulf won an IPPY award.

ALEJA TADDESSE is a writer and historian living in London. Her poetry touches on the themes of diaspora, Africa, womanhood, tradition, spirituality and religiosity. Her poems range from being introspective pieces to reimagined takes on ritualistic lore. They speak to the challenges of embracing identity on her own terms and the significance of place/belonging in a city whose diverse cultures are bound up with brutal, heavy histories of erasure and resistance. Her recent dissertation on African Liberation Movements explores grassroots, radical organising in late 20th century. She hopes to continue working on understudied histories, in particular of anti-imperialist struggles within diaspora communities in Britain and elsewhere.

NIGE TASSELL is the author of ten non-fiction books on subjects as varied as indie bands, non-league football, the Tour de France and the film *Fargo*. His latest book is *Searching For Dexys Midnight Runners*. 'The Last Supper' is the first poem he's written in almost forty years.

SARAH TERKAOUI is an Irish/Syrian poet. She has an MA in Writing Poetry and was shortlisted for the Cinnamon Press Poetry Pamphlet Award 2022, commended for the Goldsmiths Poetry Festival and the Hippocrates Poetry Prize 2021, and longlisted for the Live Canon international poetry Prize 2021. She has been published in *Black Iris, Fragmented Voices, Ink Sweat & Tears, Imposter, Persimmon Review, Porridge, Green Ink Poetry, Lucent Dreaming, Propel Magazine, The Storms, Visual Verse,* and *Dreich*.

OENONE THOMAS is a writer, psychotherapist and chocolatemaker, completing an MA in Writing Poetry at Poetry School, London. In the past year her work has appeared in publications including *Magma*, *The Alchemy Spoon*, *Propel Magazine* and *Black Iris*. She was shortlisted for the 2023 Live Canon poetry prize and longlisted for the 2023 National Poetry Competition. A selection of her poems will be published by the Newcastle Centre for the Literary Arts this Autumn.

CHRISTOPHER TRACY lives in Norwich where he works for Norfolk Record Office. His poems have appeared in *Magma*, *Lighthouse Literary Journal* and *Ink Sweat & Tears*.

KAYLA MARIE TROY is a poet from East London. Her lyrical work navigates themes of ancestry, family and loss – experimenting with political and colonial allegories to enhance her storytelling. The poem 'what I hear when sisters compare upbringings' was awarded the Out-Spoken Prize for Poetry 2023. Kayla is currently working towards her first full collection.

OLIVIA TUCK's work has been published by the Poetry Society and Broken Sleep, and in several print and online journals, including *Under the Radar*, *The Interpreter's House*, and *Perverse*. She was runner-up in the 2023 Jane Martin Poetry Prize awarded by Girton College Cambridge, and was longlisted for the 2022 Rebecca Swift Foundation Women Poets' Prize. She is an associate editor at *Tears in the Fence* and at *Lighthouse*. Her pamphlet *Things Only Borderlines Know* is out now with Black Rabbit Press.

CAT TURHAN is a poet based in North London, and her work has been published in various magazines including *The Rialto*, *Anthropocene*, *Butcher's Dog*, *Ink Sweat & Tears*, *Bath Magg*, and *Under the Radar*. She is one of the three mentees on the inaugural iteration of the Out-Spoken Emerging Poet's Mentoring Scheme. She won the 2021 Waltham Forest Competition (local category), and in 2019 and 2022 respectively was longlisted for the National Poetry Competition.

CAROLINE WIYGUL is a poet originally from the Mississippi Gulf Coast in the U.S. Her work explores the long transition from girlhood to adulthood, often through familiar ecosystems that have been transformed by climate change. This leads to lots of poems about dreams, visions of the future, and the swamp.

CARSON WOLFE is a Mancunian poet and winner of New Writing North's Debut Poetry Prize (2023). Their work has appeared with *Rattle*, *The Rumpus*, *The North*, *New Welsh Review*, *Evergreen Review*, and *The Common*. They were longlisted in The National Poetry Competition (2023) and have received awards from The Aurora Poetry Prize, The Edward Thomas Fellowship and Button Poetry.

ROJBÎN ARJEN YIĞIT is a writer and poet. She is trilingual, her poetry probes the themes of language, exile and womanhood. Amongst other places, her work has been published in *Wasafiri*, *Prototype*, *Extra Teeth* and *Propel Magazine*. Her debut poetry pamphlet, *Tongueless*, was published by Out-Spoken Press in 2024.

MEMOONA ZAHID is a writer from London. Her work has appeared in *SAND*, *Lumin Journal*, *bath magg*, and as part of The Runaways London project. She holds an MA in Poetry from The University of East Anglia.

ALIA ZAPPAROVA is an artist and writer searching for poetics of transformation in the everyday.

PROPEL MAGAZINE LIMITED
PO BOX 78744
LONDON
N11 9FG

PROPELMAGAZINE.CO.UK

WITH THANKS TO OUR PARTNERS

LEDBURY
POETRY
CRITICS